Right Place, Right Time

Also by Norman Abelson

Snapshots from a Love Affair

Love and Death in Malden (forthcoming, 2002)

Right Place, Right Time

Norman Abelson

A Kearsarge Mountain Book
Writers Publishing Cooperative

Kearsarge Mountain Books

Norman Abelson, © 2002

ISBN: 1-930149-09-03

Library of Congress CIP data available

First edition, 2001

Cover design: Mary Lou Nye
Interior: Barbara Jones

Kearsarge Mountain Books
Writers Publishing Cooperative
P.O. Box 114
Warner, N.H. 03278
rmjsc@mcttelecom.com/603-224-2654

Orders: 1-888-874-6904
www.essentialbooks.com
Printed in Canada

For Dina

Who made this book, and so many other things, possible.

Contents

MY AMERICA

THE JOY AND THE PAIN

ACKNOWLEDGMENTS

Preface

There is no there there. —Gertrude Stein

There have been many interpretations of that famous line by Ms. Stein, including suppositions that it may have been uttered under the influence of a few of her companion Alice B. Toklas's hashish-laced brownies.

I have supposed Gertrude referred to a place with no center, no core, a place of no substance. Perhaps a place lacking elan, panache, excitement, moment. Such a place would, for a person as passionate and discriminating as Ms. Stein, be dull and boring. What follows in this volume is an effort to show that there has indeed been a "there" in my life and times.

In part, I have been fortunate enough to be in the right place at the right time. In part, I have tried to open myself to the opportunities that appeared before me; I have said "yes" more often than not to the challenges.

The stories and events in this book are true, I think. Perhaps it would be better to say they are real, keeping in mind the warning addressed to memoirists by Oscar Wilde: "There is such a thing as robbing a story of its reality by trying to make it too true."

For some time, I struggled with trying to get events in order, fill in gaps, provide a flowing account. It finally occurred to me that would not—in Wilde's terms—be real. My life has happened in fits and starts; it hardly has flowed. I found, among my collection of quotations and scribbled in without attribution, this: "Memory is more like a duffel bag than a filing cabinet." So, these are not all of my stories; I do believe they are the best. They are, I feel, a good fit in these bullet-fast times as my 70th birthday has whizzed by.

Finally, I have heeded Pablo Picasso, that wondrous biographer and memoirist of the future: "In each act of creation, there is an act of destruction." In an effort (which will be seen though by some) to keep my acts of destruction to a minimum, I have, in a few instances disguised names and places.

Norman Abelson
Concord, New Hampshire

In the Beginning

March 16, 1931, dawned windy and overcast in Malden, Massachusetts. Alternately, it snowed large, wet flakes, and spit icy rain that burned against cheeks.

Twenty-seven-year-old Sophia Abelson lay in her bed in the maternity ward of the old Malden Hospital, in the working-class community five miles from Boston.

Sophia and Harry had married some 16 months earlier, in a ceremony performed by the revered Rabbi Ber Boruchoff of Congregation Beth Israel, one of several Orthodox synagogues in the city of 60,000 people, some 12,000 of them Jews.

Harry came from a line of Russian and Lithuanian Orthodox Jews who had emigrated in the early years of the 20th Century; his parents settled first in East Boston, where he was born in 1904. Soon after, they moved to a ramshackle house beside the railroad tracks along the Malden Creek.

Sophia Velleman was born in a poor suburb of London, also in 1904. Her parents were assimilated Dutch Jews whose forbears had run from the Spanish Inquisition's cruelty to the welcoming districts of The Netherlands. They moved to London just after the turn of the century where her father, Aaron, a cigar-maker, became part of the early stirrings of the modern labor movement, along with another Dutchman, Samuel Gompers. This new career led the family to come to America, where they also settled in Malden, not two miles away from the Abelsons.

Harry and Sophia met first during recess in the rock-strewn schoolyard of Daniels Elementary School. Many years later, he would recall her flirtatiousness, and she, his olive-skinned good looks. After a few years, the young friends separated when Harry ran off for an eight-year stint in the Navy, followed by a couple of years working in a cousin's auto garage in Alabama.

Sophia Velleman, like her future husband, left school after the eighth grade for work—in her case at a sewing machine as a finisher of fine ladies underwear. While Harry was traveling the world and making conquests of women with many accents, Sophia adopted the appearance and life-style of a flapper, was much sought after as a dance partner—and almost married a Harvard Dental School student.

During all those years, Harry and Sophia kept up a sporadic correspondence, and shared feelings that grew into love. Harry made his way back to Malden where he wooed and courted his former schoolmate.

Now Sophia lay alone, alternately screaming in pain and breathing easy when drugs were administered. Harry and Aaron, as was the custom, were out together getting drunk, bragging about and plotting the future of the first American grandchild about to be born into the family. I knew nothing of this story until, 50 years later, I heard it from Sophia.

On that dark winter day, when Depression still was spelled with a capital "D," I was busy inching my way down the birth canal and into the world.

It was a journey I had in common with billions of other primates, and yet heralded a life to come that was to be individual and different from any other. A life directed by the mysterious intertwining of millions of infinitesimal particles inside my brain that commanded me to take my first breath of earth's air those twenty-five thousand days ago.

These writings, as individual and idiosyncratic as that brain grew to be, and as that life has been lived, trace thoughts, opinions, feelings and events of the common yet unique human that I am.

Remembering When

Ice Man

"**H**ey, cut-cock, get inside and load on ten cakes for Perley, and eight for Morris. And don't friggn break any."

The far-from-dulcet tones of Johnny Lossano cut through my reverie. Filling my mind's eye was the vision of the neighborhood girl who had just glided by—olive-skinned, big-breasted, her behind performing an impossible hula. Sitting on the edge of the ice plant platform on a humid August afternoon, I easily imagined I was pressed against her in the narrow alley across the street, my fingers undoing three tiny buttons and moving down inside her fuzzy pink sweater. The tip of my middle finger finally made contact with the softness at the edge of her bra, and . . .

"For Chris-all-Jezus, Jew-boy, ain't y gon a-get off y ass."

It wasn't a question. I jumped up, and the fantasy popped like a soap bubble as I yanked open the outsize green door that led into the ice storage room. As I stepped from the outside 80s into the 28-degree temperature maintained to keep the ice solid, I was encapsulated in a blanket of cold. Just as I zipped up my old leather jacket and pulled down my Boston Ice Co. peaked cap, I was hit squarely on the back of the head with a baseball size ice chunk. "How many cakes y gon a-break today, Abie?"

"Fuck you, Joey." In this society, I was learning, this society of tough men doing physically taxing work, not to respond to any challenge by word or fist, was considered cowardly and bad manners. I realized that my response had been much too soft to be heard by Joey, or anyone else. "Asshole," I said to myself, in the same soft voice. I pressed the red button turning on the endless floor belt, and a loud clunk echoed through the chamber as it jerked into action. "Please don't let me break any this time," in an even softer voice. My record thus far had been lousy; every broken bar was a testament to physical weakness, a sign here of complete failure.

The belt, made of interconnected oval steel links, was set into a recess in the floor, turning at each end around circular cog wheels. The trick was to grab a 300-pound bar of ice with a pair of tongs, and twist it down to the floor, at the same time sliding it onto the moving belt in time to catch a metal lug. The ice bars would then be pushed out through a low door onto the platform where local ice men loaded their small trucks for home delivery. If I left too many lugs empty, the customers had to wait, and Lossano would scream in through the low door, "What the fuk y doin, sleepin?"

God was good, and I was successful 18 times. Still new at this inside job, I too often hit the lug sideways or dropped the huge bar to the floor, crashing it to ice knives and splinters, while I scurried to keep it from crushing my toes. When this happened, Lossano—whose way of expressing satisfaction was a jolting punch on the shoulder—would go ballistic. "I got a-friggn account for erry friggn cake made in this muthern plant, you dumb kike. This is comn out-ay split. If y fatha dint work for this company, I'd fire yr ass. No, I'd fukkn kill y."

Dark, short, bald, Lossano had a voice like a crow's. His face was a landscape of deep pocks, and he walked with his feet splayed, like a penguin. His speech was littered with ethnic and religious slurs and curses; and he was innovative. Never before nor since have I been referred to as cut-cock, a reference to every male Jew's first surgery. But, taken all together, he wasn't a bad guy. When, later in the summer, I began to carry my own weight, I got punched in the shoulder much more often than I was assaulted by anti-Semitic verbiage.

Johnny had worked at Boston Ice since he was a kid, and was proud of making his way up to platform man in overall charge of this ice-making factory. In this world, the only measurements for status and accomplishment were toughness and strength. This was a new challenge for me, one Lossano and the other men at this plant already had met.

That summer of 1951, my twentieth, found me, I see now in retrospect, in the midst of depression. But my brooding and spending time alone were taken by some close to me, including my mother, as an as-yet unrealized artistic temperament. Others, notably my father, saw my behavior as immature clap-trap, a continuation of my irresponsible teen years.

It was true that thus far my life had had all the direction of a pinball, bouncing aimlessly and by chance from one electric bumper to another.

After barely squeaking through high school, all attitude and anger, I landed at Northeastern University with absolutely no idea why, other than that my friend, Donnie, had chosen that school. But our friendship cooled as he, ambitious, took his studies seriously, while I fell in (actually pushed my way in) with a group of World War II veterans who were still at loose ends, and using a free education as a kind of last, long vacation.

It was right up my alley. Opening the scholastic day with 9 a.m. Bloody Marys at the nearby Elliot Lounge. Skipping class, chain-smoking and coffee in the Commons. Our big round table was the center of attention, and by invitation only. The leaders of the group, Burton Price and Frankie Carroll, had taken to me, and I was their grateful tyro. Burton was the son of a wealthy trucking company founder in Somerville; Frankie was the oldest son in an Irish-American working class family that lived in the section of Brookline where John F. Kennedy was born.

After three semesters of this high life, the down side of which was my dismal academic record and resultant guilt, I decided to quit. My father insisted that I personally inform the dean and each of my professors of my decision, so that I could end my college life "like a man." Feeling more like a failure than a man, I did his bidding and left, regretting only leaving behind my pals and the zaftig Vivian, whose wish of a lifetime together for us was doomed anyway after her father grilled me about my financial condition (I didn't have one), and my intentions, which chilled when he promised that for a respectable son-in-law there would be a place in his wholesale butcher business.

No longer a college man, I lost not only my status but also free room-and-board. Dad said I had to get a job and to give my mother at least $10 a week toward family expenses. My maternal grandfather, Aaron, was an organizer for the American Federation of Labor, and had unionized the Lewis Candy Factory, just a couple of miles from our house. He told me he had set up a job interview with one of the owners.

Pledging to start anew and with resolve, I put on my best—and only—good clothes: Striped brown-and-white tie, tan corduroy jacket and dark brown slacks. I started to walk to the factory telling myself not to expect too much to start, probably some menial office job.

Surprise one was being met not by an owner but some low-level manager who wasn't even wearing a tie. Surprise two was learning what my new job was: Floor sweeper. He led me to a locker where I traded my finery for an unpressed set of dark green coveralls.

My hirer made it clear the job was a favor to Aaron who he called "a hell of guy for a union organizer." He handed me a wide push-broom and disappeared without further direction. I was feeling demeaned and embarrassed but, what the hell, I'd go find a floor to sweep. Exact pictures of the factory have blurred with time, but I recall there were several floors where a couple of hundred women were doing what it took to make chocolates.

The women, most of them Italian-Americans from the Edgeworth neighborhood where the factory was sited, were tough in act and word. Their language was equal to any I would hear at the ice plant. Each outfitted in coveralls, their hair was tucked under snoods. As I walked by their work stations, pushing my broom, they would call out to me— "Ay, wyl-yo, what you got for me? Wanna suck on my chocolate?"— and occasionally reach out to grab my crotch or behind. What should have been a dream come true for a sex-deprived young man, scared the hell out of me. I left after two weeks, enhancing my quitter image at home, and resumed brooding.

"I talked to Johnny Lossano today, and he's willing to take you on at the Cambridge plant," my father told me one night when he returned from work. "But there's no platform work. You're going to have to be inside, handling the ice." There was a pause, and the words I knew were coming: "This is a favor to me. Don't let me down."

While the nationwide use of ice as a cooling agent was on the wane by that year, its manufacture was still big business. Boston Ice was a subsidiary of the American Ice Co. of New York, which had plants all over the Northeast, and beyond. The firm also was big in the sale of coal, coke, kerosene and wood, supplying homes, businesses and industries with heating and power needs.

While those supplies seem like ancient history today, I still can recall the deafening sounds of banging and scraping as a ton of coal shot out of the truck, down a steel chute, through a small ground-level window, and crashed with a thud onto our cellar floor. And I remember the weight of the coal when, as a small kid, I toted it on a shovel as big as me from the bin and dumped it into the raging fire inside our furnace.

I still can hear the swishing sound when I carried the five-gallon kerosene container, its narrow metal handle digging into my fingers and palms, up three flights to keep our kitchen stove going. As unpleasant as those daily chores were, there was something reassuring about the direct relation between the tasks and their results—keeping warm in a frigid Massachusetts winter, and having your food cooked.

I also recall that when there was a coal delivery, clouds of fine black dust were thrown up. In the early days, my dad would return to our home after a 12-hour day working on the coal truck, his clothes and body covered with the dust. But when he died of lung cancer some years later, it was attributed only to his cigarette smoking. I guess it doesn't matter whether it was the Camels or coal dust that did it.

Our two ice delivery men, Perley Vogeler, a taciturn Nova Scotian, and Morris Gould, a dour Russian-Jewish immigrant who spat a lot, would lug a hundred-pound slice of ice glued to rubber mats on their backs, upstairs, and slide it into our modern-looking ice chest. Long after even my poorest friends had electric refrigerators, I still was emptying the water pan kept under the chest to collect the melt-off.

Out of loyalty to his employer, my father would not allow an electric fridge into the house. Like Johnny Lossano, joining Boston Ice as a young man, Dad had worked his way up, in his case to district superintendent, and finally an office job at Boston headquarters. His loyalty was repaid this way: After more than forty years, and just two years short of retirement, he was, unceremoniously and without explanation, fired. Some Jew-hating bigots also had made their way up in the company, unfortunately higher up than Dad. It cost him most of his pension and all of his dignity. Soon there was a used Gibson electric refrigerator in our kitchen.

It was a good many years before that unhappy close to my father's career, however, when I showed up for work at Lossano's plant on First Street in Cambridge. The occasion was not without its irony. Since I was 15, I had worked summers for Boston Ice. Always it was assumed by all that these were school vacation jobs, and that later I would go to college and move on to a more "expected" career. Well, now I had failed at the expected path, and working as an ice man was the only career I had. The edge I had held as the first-born grandchild and later as the first in my immediate family to enter college, was gone. It was mustard-cutting time.

My earlier days as an ice man were more care-free and studded with memories, some more pleasant than others. When I worked in my home town of Malden, I would walk the couple of miles to the plant in the still-dark coolness, and open at 5 AM. The plant was located along the Malden Creek and the railroad tracks, and across the yard from a three-decker tenement that was home to three good looking prostitutes with whom I shared some salacious conversations—and nothing else. When my tour was over, there was plenty of time to hop the streetcar and enjoy long and languid afternoons dozing and tanning on Revere Beach.

Other job sites were less idyllic. The plant in Day Square, East Boston, was home to a pretty rowdy gang of toughs who would dive naked off the rotting pier at the rear of the plant into a filthy, oil slick inlet. I always kept a sharp ice pick in a leather sheath at my belt, should I need it for self-protection. The worst that happened was name calling and rock tossing.

But wherever I worked, the pay was great. Often I raked in a net of more than $100 a week, a fortune in those days, which bankrolled some pretty fancy dates with some pretty fancy girls for me and my more impecunious pals. A healthy portion of the spoils came from secret side deals, the income from which was kept in a kitty and split up at the end of each week.

Money poured in from selling 50-pound bags of shaved ice over the platform to folks who used it mostly for chilling beer at parties. The price ranged from 50 cents to a dollar, depending on how expensive the customer's car looked. The buyers assumed we took chunks of clean ice and ran them through a crushing machine. They were wrong. Ice cost money. In truth, we shoveled up accumulated, and not overly sanitary, ice frozen to the floor of the plant. Talk about low overhead!

Just as lucrative was the ice cube trade. One of the jobs at the plant was to bag 50-pounds of ice cubes for sale to restaurants, hotels and bars. By short-weighting each bag by an unnoticeable few pounds,we would "own" a large supply by the end of each day, and then be in business for ourselves. Other schemes involved coming into ownership of gallons of kerosene and fuel oil by bypassing the meters.

Once I asked my father whether he took part in this chicanery when he worked the plants. He just smiled. He never asked me, his straight-arrow and slightly self-righteous son, how I justified my part in taking the money. Just as well; my case was weak. I told myself that I didn't want to be seen as a wimp who would blow the whistle.

My years as an ice man saw me through rights of passage and feelings of accomplishment that I wouldn't trade, in spite of the moments of sheer terror. It turned out to be the only time in my life that I earned a living by doing manual labor. Never since have I felt as productive. Never since has a paycheck seemed as well earned or satisfying.

For that matter, never since has food tasted so good. Getting out of bed at 4 AM left neither time nor desire for breakfast. But by 6:30, when one of the guys would go out for food, I was ravenous. My breakfast never changed: Three huge, hot, bright yellow corn muffins, dripping with butter, and two tall containers of muddy coffee. Work would stop, and the entire crew would gather outside in the cool early morning air. There we sat, me and half a dozen tough guys, steam shooting up from our cardboard coffee cups, eating in complete silence—the only silence of the day.

By lunchtime, the day had come alive. It was noisier and more convivial. We'd sit on the edge of the platform, eyes alert for passing women to be ogled and hooted at. There was a lot of chatter, laughing, jostling and trading of food. Even Lossano would join in occasionally, though he never ate with us. My lunch, typically, included four thick sandwiches brought from home, washed down with a quart of chocolate milk. We always capped off the hour with a trip across the street to the little grocery/luncheonette for a couple of ice cream bars, a chunk of apple pie, and punch-out chances on a game board that seemed to have no winning numbers.

The ritual called "warm up" took me a while to get used to. Stashed away strategically in corners of the cold plant were half-pint bottles of cheap whiskey. The first round of these stomach warmers was downed at about 6 AM. While I was a pretty good drinker, even at my young age, gut-stinging booze on an empty stomach at that hour was pretty hard to swallow. But the option of being seen as a wimp was more daunting, so swallow it I did, and with a minimum of gagging.

Because I was, at least at first, so physically inferior, I compensated by considering myself the intellectual superior of my fellow workers. This theory got knocked in the head the day I was assigned to fill ice cube bags. Standing for eight hours in front of tall bins, filling bag after bag, was repetitious and boring. And what was worse, I would have to stand beside that strange guy who always wore a brown shirt and leather tie to work, and mumbled to himself constantly.

This guy's not only weird, he's stupid, I thought as I took my place beside him. But now, for the first time, I was able to hear his muttering. It was large chunks of Shakespeare he was reciting from memory. "That's terrific, what you're doing," I said to him, patronizingly. He turned to me, smiled, bowed his head slightly in response, and returned to his work, and to his recitation. I can still see his face—Roman nose, eyes slightly bulging, thick lips—but I'm damned if I can remember his name.

A name I'll never forget is Joe Gill, a one-time professional wrestler. Joe was built like a block of granite, and was fond of inviting people to punch him anywhere above the belt, as hard as they could. He had once served a few years in prison for hitting a man a little too hard in a barroom brawl—and killing him. Normally, Joe was a happy and benign man. So it was confusing that he continued to pick on me, challenge me, administer painful lessons.

Early one morning he locked me in the tiny bathroom; first, though, he had thrown an ammonia-soaked rag into the sink. Ammonia was used a lot in the ice-manufacturing process, so we got used to the smell in an open space. Also, it was a fast way to sober up if you came to work still a bit under the weather. But in that cramped room, the air quickly became saturated, and my eyes began to water. I started to cough and choke, and dropped to the floor searching for clean air. Just as I thought I would lose consciousness, Joe pulled open the door and dragged me outside.

On another occasion, as I sat in the office chair drinking coffee, Joe picked me up, chair and all, carried me outside and dropped me off the platform several feet to the concrete below. It felt like my neck bone had been fused into my tailbone, but I forced myself to laugh it off. Other times he would wrap me in a bear hug and toss me around like a rag doll.

Figuring I had nothing to lose, one day I asked: "What the hell have you got against me, Joe?" He laughed. "Jeez, kid, I really like you, and you're pretty damn spunky." Then his voice dropped as he added, "You know your old man and me are friends; he's been damn good to me. He said you were kind a soft and for me to toughen you up." I told Joe I'd had enough toughening up, and from that day on, the hazing stopped.

After a couple of summers on the job, I was invited to join the Teamsters union, which represented us as warehousemen. It was another step toward acceptance, to be evidenced by the union pin I could stick in my cap. Our shop steward, a man named McQueeney, swore me in in the presence of my co-workers. Years later I became an active member of the American Newspaper Guild, but it wasn't the same. I still have my Teamsters card and pin tucked away in one of my boxes of junk from the past.

My brightest memory occurred just before I left the Cambridge plant, and the ice business, for the last time, to begin a new career in journalism. At the close of one of my last workdays, Al, the senior man at the plant, came up to me and asked: "What y doing after work?" I said I was heading home. "Well, me and the guys would like for y to join us for a few shooters."

I had given up hope of being invited to join them after work at the local bar. I thought I understood why. These men knew there was little chance that I would live out my work life in the plant, as they were destined to do. So they weren't going to share any part of their private lives with me. Again I had misunderstood—this time their way of taking the measure of a man. They had been waiting for me to earn an invitation.

All those months, while ridiculing me verbally, they frequently covered for me, did part of my work, until I got up to speed. The invitation was the signal that I could hold my own now, that finally I was a peer.

So there I was with my belly up against a long mahogany bar, downing straight shots of rye, followed by long cool draughts of beer. Laughing and drinking and shooting pool with them, I suddenly realized I was going to miss these men one hell of a lot. They were not so bathetic as to toast me or even to mention my departure.

There were no final good-byes when, pretty happy and pretty drunk, I slammed on my Boston Ice Co. cap and headed dizzily for the door. No good-byes unless you count Lossano's parting words.

"See y Abe," he croaked from the far end of the bar, and added, knowingly: "Maybe."

Smoldering Secrets

These days I enjoy an occasional cigar. It relaxes me and, after all, both my grandfather and great-grandfather were cigar makers, and prodigious smokers of their products. I award myself a long cigar at the close of a productive day of writing, or as a reward for keeping to my diet.

But I remember back to a time when a stogie was administered to me as a harsh punishment, and was anything but pleasurable. My best friend, Charlie, and I had been caught smoking first when he was 12 and I was 11. Charlie's father had beaten his backside three colors, and my father, who had just completed a night course in psychology, made me smoke a big, black cigar.

Undeterred, we returned to our bad habit, and now, a year later, Charlie's sister had found out and squealed. There would be hell to pay. Damn Charlie's sister! She must have seen us behind the old Judson School. That's where we used to sit—on the black, steel fire escape in back of the Judson School—and smoke.

Recent graduates, we felt at home in the tiny wooden schoolhouse. Judson had four rooms, four old-maid teachers, rock-covered yards and the foulest-smelling boys' room in the East. But it provided great cover as we puffed on our Twenty Grands, at 12 cents a package, the strongest cigarettes on the market.

In our working class neighborhood, youngsters didn't get an allowance. If you wanted money of your own you either went to work—which we both did the next year—or you "appropriated" things of value. In our case, we stole store bottles from backhalls. Few people on our street had milk delivered—most bought it as needed at Tesler's, the corner variety store. Each bottle was returnable for a nickel. Three bottles got us a pack of Twenty Grands and a half dozen books of paper matches.

When the supply was low, we'd bring in one bottle, and the old man who ran the dingy corner market would illegally break open a package and slowly count out in Yiddish "Ein, zwei, drei, vier, funf . . ." carefully dropping five of the ovals and five wooden matches into my hand.

But now Charlie's mother knew and promised to tell Charlie's father when he came home from the die-making factory. And I knew Mr. Perry would tell my father. We talked it over in our blanket tent next to the chestnut tree in Charlie's backyard. We decided to run away. No beatings, no cigars this time.

Since my house was empty, I was put in charge of gathering supplies. I filled my knapsack with a can of corn, three oranges, four potatoes, a can opener, my Boy Scout knife and a canteen full of water. Charlie told me he had emptied our cache in his cellar and had half a pack of Twenty Grands and some matches. Our cash assets totaled seven cents.

Deciding not to leave any notes, we told our non-smoking friend, Stanley, of our plan. We swore him to secrecy regarding our destination, but said he could tell our parents we were safe if they seemed worried.

Our hideout was a heavily wooded area surrounding a small pond, about four miles from our neighborhood. It was summer, the sun was shining, and Charlie and I felt good as we walked through Malden Square. We made faces in store windows, swore out loud and challenged a couple of kids to a fight—and then ran like hell when it looked like they might accept our invitation.

We got to our hideaway in late afternoon, and spent the first half-hour in surveillance, making sure there weren't any spies around. Then we dined on cold corn, warm oranges and tepid water. We saved the potatoes for the next meal. What's more natural after good food than a smoke? We lit up happily, paying no notice to the match dropped into the dry grass at the edge of the woods.

Suddenly there was a flare-up. We both went to stamp it out. But one of us—I can't remember which—said, "Let's let it burn for a minute, and see what happens."

Just then, a gust of wind came up, and the fingers of flame spread, first to a clump of dry bushes and then, almost instantly, to the small trees which edged the woodland. We tore off our polo shirts and began to beat at the perimeter of the fire. We filled empty tin cans with water from the pond and tried to douse the flames. Nothing helped. It seemed as though the whole forest was ablaze.

It was beginning to get dark and, panicking, we ran to the street to flag down a car. When one finally stopped, we told the driver about the fire and asked him to get the fire department. Long minutes passed before we heard the bells and sirens.

Two pumpers and a fire department car pulled up close to the blaze. As the hoses were being unwound, one of the firefighters said, "Okay, boys, we'll take over now," and sent us back near the park entrance, where we sat silent on a low stone wall. We must have presented quite a heroic sight—two small boys beating at a forest fire, sweaty and faces streaked black from the soot. But we were feeling anything but heroic.

"Jeez, we're goin' to get killed," Charlie said to me. I could only nod in agreement, wondering what hell my father would come up with to spoil the rest of the summer.

What seemed like an inferno to us was not really that big. The fire-fighters had it under control in no time; all that remained was the hiss of water on sizzling embers, and a lot of smoke.

The lieutenant in charge walked toward us, stripping off his rubber coat. Charlie and I didn't doubt something bad was coming.

"You kids were real brave," he said, "but don't ever try that again. You could have gotten in real trouble. C'mon, I'll give you a ride home in my car." The next thing we knew, we were tooling home in a red fire car, pretty confused.

Our families, worried when we were not home to dinner, had squeezed the truth out of Stanley, and were talking together in a small huddle outside our adjoining houses when we pulled up.

I began to feel a glimmer of hope as the lieutenant told our folks how brave we had been. By the time he finished, the fireman saved Charlie and me from punishment—at least for the immediate future. I got a warmed-over supper and was put to bed by my mother, who even kissed me goodnight.

Actually, the punishment never came, because the next day the local newspaper had a front-page story about the fire, which told of "the heroic efforts of two Malden youngsters who tried to extinguish the blaze."

My First Best Friend

When I was 7 years old, my best friend was an 85-year-old Dutchman named Isaac Peekel. He was also my great grandfather.

In the closing years of the Great Depression, we lived all together in a six-room flat, nine people from four generations of the family. Even as a kid, I was aware of the reason we lived crowded like that. The rent was $36 a month, and no one in the family could swing it alone.

So Grandpa Peekel and my mother's parents moved in, and paid their share. Then my uncle's wife died in childbirth, so he and the baby came in to live with my parents, my brother, me and the rest.

From this crowd Grandpa Peekel and I emerged as special buddies. Of course we loved each other, but there was more to this bond. Maybe it was about the very young and the very old not being listened to, not having their opinions valued.

Grandpa Peekel emigrated in the early part of the century, when he already was in his middle years and had outlived three wives. By trade he was a cigar maker, and for many years he plied his craft hand-rolling the rich, brown leaves in the front window of a tobacco emporium along Boston's Washington Street. By the time I came along, he already was retired.

Grandpa Peekel was a man of varied tastes. He relished a good cigar, loved a plateful of boiled potatoes and reveled in a hot game of penny poker. He was a shrewd player, and not above betting his pennies on a bluff now and again. And when he lost, he was not above a little profanity, in Dutch, of course.

"Godverdomme," he would say, throwing his cards on the table. But even in his anger there was always a twinkle in his eyes. And his worn old face would screw up into a mock displeasure when I would ask: "What does that mean, Grandpa?"

"It means time for the young one to go to bed. Tomorrow we go to the moving pictures, if you sleep in 10 minutes." Then, turning to my mother, his granddaughter, he would add: "You people know nothing of raising a child, Sofchia. In the old country the little ones did not stand around the card table. You spoil him."

The truth, known to all, was that he was spoiling me. My parents knew all this, but as I look back those 60 years, I can see they loved Grandpa Peekel and me too much ever to separate us. There was a time when the family talked of sending him to an old age home, each relative contributing what he could toward the room and board. I think I was about 7 or 8 at the time. Grandpa would not have complained about being sent away; he was always apologetic about "intruding."

But my parents would have none of it, and for this I always will be grateful to them. After all, he was my first best friend and my first teacher. I remember that by the time I was 7, he had read me every volume of the Book of Knowledge, cover to cover. He brought coal mines in England, the diamond fields of South Africa, the wheat fields of Kansas alive to me.

Once, when we came to the section on Holland, there was a picture of a quaint bridge. He put aside the book and told me of a policeman in his hometown who had arrested his own, slightly intoxicated, father, who had thrown his coat over a bridge. He laughed until the tears came to his eyes.

We shared another love: the movies. Grandpa Peekel was a poor man. He got the equivalent of about $30 a month in pension from the Dutch government. A portion of it would go to my mother to help with the household expenses. Some went for cigars and pipe tobacco and his other personal needs. Whatever was left was for our entertainment.

"Well boy," he would say in Dutch (I could understand the language then), "the pension is here. Tomorrow we go to the moving pictures." He loved the cops-and-robbers and cowboy movies, so we always went to the same theater-the Orpheum-which played only such thrillers.

How proud I was walking down to Malden Square at the side of the old man, especially when the traffic cop would stop all the cars for us and give Grandpa Peekel a salute. That was the first time I can remember feeling important. My heart melts now as I can see him digging deep into his leather purse, pulling out a dime and nickel for the tickets, and always another precious nickel for my candy.

He died soon after his 87th birthday. It was late one night when noises in the house roused me from sleep. Dr. Hoberman was there. An ambulance, horribly frightening to a young boy, was backed up to the door and two white-clad attendants took Grandpa Peekel out on a stretcher. I just got a glimpse of his face as they carried him through the door. I yelled out his name, but he didn't answer.

It was the last time I ever saw him. He died soon after reaching the hospital. The doctors said it was some kind of blood clot, and old age. My mother tried to assure me he had not suffered, and that he had lived a rich, full life. But I was inconsolable.

He returned to our house in a coffin, and I was sent next door to stay until after the funeral. My parents told me years later they did not want my last memory of Grandpa Peekel to be a sad one. But, against orders, I peeked through the window of the neighbor's house, and, my hot tears dropping on the windowsill, I saw a mahogany casket with silver handles carried down my front steps and pushed into a black hearse, which then made its way slowly down Stearns Street and out of my sight.

Teen Dating: Gettin' None

"The best thing about the '60s is that they freed me from my underwear." So said a young friend of mine as we were comparing our teen dating experiences.

Her words set me to thinking about how different my experiences were a quarter-century before the liberating '60s. Often the challenge then wasn't whether the young woman was willing, or even how to get her to be, but the difficulty of just getting to it. Many of the girls in my set were all wrapped up in chastity-preserving layers by mothers fighting to keep their treasures pure for some as-yet-unmet medical student.

I remember, especially, one winter night when I rode a trolley for an hour and a half to a Boston suburb for a date with a young woman who, on earlier trysts, had seemed—in the vernacular of the day— "warm for my form." After some begging from the daughter, her mother gave us use of her car. She set an 11 PM curfew and enough admonitions against going parking to drain the desire from a monkey during mating season.

Nonetheless, twenty minutes later there we were, parked beside the reservoir behind St. Ignatius Church. It was a storied spot where a couple of my buddies claimed to have broken through the barriers set up by mothers who had burned into their princesses' brains the then-acceptable adage: He won't buy the cow if he gets the milk free. In my unrequited dating experiences up to then, not only was the milk as rare and costly as fine champagne, it was quite often beyond physical reach.

Here's what I mean. In the cold weather there was always the damnable mouton coat. Made of sheepskin fashioned to look like beaver, mouton was the outer armor. It hid the charms of the most curvaceous young lady beneath fur so thick that a hand roaming from the outside had no clue whether the shape on the inside was akin to Marilyn Monroe or an anorexic model. And to make it worse, there lurked somewhere an evil and wealthy seamstress who, on mothers' orders, sewed buttonholes just a tad smaller than the bulky buttons.

So even on the coldest nights it was necessary to take off one's gloves for the demanding tactile tasks ahead. (Always there was the hope of finding a warm landing place for hands later.) Well, on this night, by the time the last of the mouton buttons was conquered, along with the time-consuming, but then obligatory demurrals of the girl, my hands were numb, white ice chunks.

After using one frozen pinky as a lever, I released the bottom button and pulled open the mouton coat, feeling no less triumphant than our forefather, Moses, must have at the parting of the Red Sea.

But now I was faced with the second line of defense: a breastplate consisting of a two-piece cashmere sweater set, with lines of tiny pearl buttons secured by tight little loops of cotton. I began blowing on my frozen fingers, facing a task to test the dexterity of a brain surgeon.

As the curfew neared, decisions had to be made. I opted for just a momentary stop at the barely discernible upper curves, still hidden beneath two sweaters, a slip and a bra. My hopes for greater victories below turned quickly to dust. As I moved my hands south, I met an impenetrable navel-to-mid-thigh girdle that was tighter than a Speedo on a fat guy.

Don't tell me that my date's devious mother, dreaming of winters on Miami Beach and a lifetime of free medical care, wasn't aware that by the time things had advanced this far, one hapless young man, his brain swirling with passion, but his fine motor skills destroyed by the cold, would sense defeat.

She was right. My energy, among other things, began to flag. With time running out, efforts to mount the battlements seemed futile. My fingers were no longer able to distinguish between skin and fabric. Streams of water dripped down the car windows as the vapor, a visual sign of heavy breathing and all that meant, began to disappear, and the inside temperature plummeted.

It was over. I laughed nervously. Embarrassed, she sort of giggled and began to rebutton the coat. (Why did it seem so much easier to button than unbutton it?) She drove me to the trolley stop and gave me a kiss that her mother would have approved of.

As I climbed aboard the Lake Street-Commonwealth car for the long ride home, I began to construct, for my buddies the next day, a feasible story that would somewhat protect the girl's reputation while, at the same time, enhancing mine.

One thing I knew. I sure as hell wasn't going to tell them the truth: that I rode the trolley all the way home wearing a condom—unused.

Saturday Adventure

Air conditioning was barely known in those days. The coolest—and the best—place to be on a Saturday afternoon in summer was the inside of a movie house.

It was a situation always filled with anticipation, going to the movies. Two ten-year-olds, on a carefree jaunt down Ferry Street, cutting across Irving onto Main. My friend, Charlie, and I, clad only in shorts, polo shirts and Converse sneakers, walking along nearly empty city streets while the mid-July sun beat down from its noontime high. Outside thermometers were registering in the top of the '90s.

There was only one sure way to cool down on the way to the movies. If we were lucky, we would come upon an ice truck parked outside a tenement, or moving slowly along a side street, checking front windows for the cardboard signs announcing the need for the chilly product. Of course, the best deal was to meet a truck as the ice-man was chipping a 50-pound chunk from one of the huge 300-pound blocks that were manufactured in the Boston Ice Company plant on Phillips Court. That was an opportunity to obtain a long, fresh sliver of ice, clean and unmelted. But even an older piece, slightly melted and covered with soft splinters of wood from the rotting bottom of the truck bed, were darn good. You just had to know how to keep from swallowing the first few licks, and spit out the splinters.

The whole Saturday adventure was too exciting a prospect for me to eat lunch, so my mother would prepare a matinee special, packed in a crumpled brown paper bag: two sandwiches and an apple. But these were not ordinary sandwiches.

They were made on fresh, puffy Wonder Bread, one side slathered with thick oily peanut butter from Kennedy's Dairy Store and the other smeared with a deep purple layer of the world's sweetest grape jelly. The apple was for therapeutic purposes to offset the sweet sandwiches and a gigantic Mr. Goodbar I would purchase with the extra nickel that was jangling in the left front pocket of my shorts, along with the 11 cents for admission (10 cents plus a 1-cent war tax; this was in the early '40s).

We never decided in advance which theater we would attend; that would have spoiled the anticipation. The choice rested, usually, between the Orpheum, located on Main Street next to Meyer Baker's clothing store, and the Mystic, up on Pleasant Street near the old red brick YMCA building. Every once-in-a-while, when there was an especially good horror moving playing, we would trek all the way up to the Strand, which sat close to an overhead railroad bridge.

But the Mystic or the Orpheum were the odds-on favorites for at least three reasons: They were the cheapest, they had kid's shows on Saturday, and they lasted the longest. We generally got to Malden Square early so we could assess where best to get our 11-cents worth. We always used the same route. First, we would stop outside the Orpheum, check out all the posters and engage in a bit of intelligence gathering from the lady in the ticket booth. Then we would walk up to the Mystic and carry out the same ritual.

Once a choice was made, we lost no time getting inside; there were important decisions ahead, and they needed to be made before the show started. There was the matter of seating. We could sit down front, in the first couple of rows, and get a wonderfully distorted and scary view. We could sit in the back row so no tough kids could bean us from behind. Or we could sit high in the balcony and toss spit balls or pieces of popcorn into the path of the projection beam, where they would light up momentarily like shooting stars. Not an easy decision.

But first there was the business of selecting a candy bar. While it was fun to speculate on the many choices open to a kid with a nickel, I remained loyal to Mr. Goodbar, a one-pound chunk of chocolate, loaded with peanuts. While my sack of provisions may seem heavy in retrospect, it must be remembered that the average fare in those days was a lot different from the hour-and-a-half "quickie" movie experience today. A Saturday matinee consisted of all or most of the following:

1. News or current events. ("Pathe News" or "Time Marches On")

2. At least one cartoon. ("Popeye" was my favorite.)

3. Coming Attractions.

4. Humorous subject. ("Our Gang" or "The Three Stooges," e.g.)

5. A travelogue (such as "Canoeing down the Mysterious Congo")

6. A serial. ("Flash Gordon" and "Dick Tracy" were favorites.)

7. The second feature. (Which were called "B" films.)

8. The main feature. (Often no better than the second feature.)

Finally, the time came. Already munching on my first sandwich, I would scrunch down in my seat as the lights went down and the screen lit up with the first magic images. And there in the cool darkness of a building in the center of Malden, two friends were carried away for a few hours from the heat of the day and the realities of their young lives. The only decision immediately ahead was whether to risk the wrath of their parents by staying through two shows.

Home Again

There, lying on the kitchen table in my mother's home, was the Malden Evening News. I went to Malden with some frequency, but almost always it was a hurried trip between my home in New Hampshire and my mother's up on Belmont Hill. Little time for reading newspapers or reflecting on my growing up years in Malden.

But now, as I read a front page story about pupils at Lincoln School collecting money to help spruce up the Statue of Liberty, I am moved back to the time when I was a student at Lincoln Junior High School in the early '40s. We lived then in a six-room flat, great-grandfather Isaac Peekel, grandparents Aaron and Sarah Velleman, parents Harry and Sophia, brother Stephen and I. Other great-grandparents lived minutes away, with assorted aunts and uncles and scads of cousins all within shouting distance.

It was then what is today called—with perhaps too much gentility— a mixed-ethnic neighborhood. In most houses, one could hear some accent or another and, while some people were a bit better off than others, a family was considered to be doing darn well if it had a car, money for the movies once in a while, and vacationed for a week on the northern reaches of Revere Beach in July.

I can remember Gene Lovins and Harold Shwartz, and Junie Duvall who was good on the Hawaiian guitar. Jakie Shoulder and Jo Jo Piccarelli. Around the corner Stanley Rosenblatt and Barney Scardino, who moved to Escondido, California, leaving his grieving shepherd, Butch, behind to die of a broken heart. A few streets up lived Miltie Madnick and Jerry Bornstein, and closer, Jimmie Santosuosso.

Charlie Perry was my next-door best buddy; we played under a stretched out blanket on his front porch, eating his mother's home-made white bread layered with sandwich spread. Florrie Perry baked the best apple pie and doughnuts that God would allow on earth. On payday at the die factory, we would wait at the corner of Stearns and Holyoke for Charlie's father, Joe, who would reach down into the pocket of his work pants and fish out a penny for each of us. My Dad was no less generous when payday rolled around at Boston Ice Co., after he had pulled his DeSoto into the cracked cement driveway between our two houses.

Down on the corner was Tesler's Variety Store where, for a penny, one could choose from a handful of hard candy, a very small sherbet (more like an ice) in a paper cup, or—if no parents were in the vicinity—one Twenty Grands cigarette and a wooden match. The cigarette was stashed and smoked later in privacy.

When we could muster up a few more pennies, usually by stealing "store" bottles from back steps, we would split a large bottle of Y.D. orange soda, made down at Louis Newman's bottling plant. In fact, the two Malden tastes that have remained with me through the years, are Y.D. orange soda and fresh-baked dark rye bread, bought after midnight for 12 cents at Malitsky's Bakery on Franklin Street, and eaten steaming hot while strolling through Suffolk Square.

Assemblies at Lincoln Junior High were not modeled around career days or psycho-social "how-to" programs for attaining financial and emotional nirvana. The times I remember most vividly in the auditorium were when Principal Jim Cronin would trot out some unfortunate who had recently completed a stretch at reform school. The poor soul (one, I recall, was a nice guy named Benny) was left quaking and alone, behind a microphone on a huge stage, ordered to scare the hell out of the audience with tales of dry bread and whippings to lay one's bones bare. What left the most imprint on me, perhaps ironically, is that this young man—whose survival in the streets was tied to his toughness—was literally embarrassed to tears, finally sobbing out his admonishment that we should all "be good," especially in school.

Now as I place the Malden News back on my mother's table and prepare for the ride back to New Hampshire, I contemplate how many things are different. My great grandparents and grandparents, long gone. My father and Charlie's parents, gone. The kids on the block scattered to who-knows where. Tesler's gone. Louis Newman gone. Malitsky's Bakery and Suffolk Square as we knew it, gone too.

But the memories of my childhood in Malden remain with me, as fresh and warm as a chunk of Malitsky's dark rye, eaten with joy and zest by a young man for whom all things were possible.

Radio Days

On a chill fall night some 75 years ago, commercial radio was born when a voice barely audible through the static announced from station KDKA in Pittsburgh that Warren G. Harding had been elected President of the United States.

The voices moved—miraculously—through the air. They were captured, at first, on crude crystal sets in a few hundred homes. Then they made their way into millions of houses, and connected people everywhere as never before.

I remember when radio, as we know it, was in its very early years. For people today, traveling at breakneck speed along the internet, it must be difficult to imagine the impact radio had on all of us—adults and kids—when it became part of family life in America.

The first two radios in my home were spectacular and mysterious. The mahogany floor model in the parlor had a huge speaker, and its array of vacuum tubes and wires pulled in stations even from other countries. The table-top model was perched on an open cabinet above the sink in our kitchen, the room in which the family gathered evenings. It was shaped like a cathedral, with pointed spires rising from the corners.

When the championship fights came on, especially those involving my dad's hero, the great Joe Louis, my job was to stand on a chair and squeeze the antenna wire, an action that somehow increased the volume. The roar of the crowd, the excited voices of the commentators, the grunts of the combatants. Don't let anyone tell you that you cannot "see" radio. As poet Wallace Stevens wrote: "Imagination is the one reality in this imagined world."

So while I sometimes cannot remember what I had for breakfast, I cannot forget my early radio days going back more than half a century. I even remember my mom's soap operas.

There was Ma Perkins, who ran a small-town lumber yard, and in her spare time, solved all the problems in the community. And Mary

Noble, backstage wife, whose love life made Elizabeth Tayor's seem like a walk in the park.

For us kids there were the afternoon adventure shows like "Terry and the Pirates," "Sky King," and "Jack Armstrong, AAAAALLLLLL American Boy!" Saturday mornings were a treasure trove for kids, especially "Let's Pretend," a wondrous half-hour of story telling.

Just about every night featured good, clean comedy. Jack Benny. Fred Allen. Eddie Cantor. Fibber Magee and Mollie. Abbott and Costello, with their hilarious "Who's on First" routine.

And there was drama both to enchant and scare the daylights out of you. The Lux Radio Theater. Grand Central Station. I Love a Mystery.

The NBC Radio Orchestra was world renowned. President Roosevelt's fireside chats put to rest, at least for a while, the woes and worries of a nation still reeling from the Great Depression.

What is left of any of this world, and there is precious little, is broadcast over public radio. Radio had perhaps more of an impact on my imagination even than books. But while it was with us morning, noon and night, it never was intrusive and all encompassing, like television.

While the radio was on, my parents would play cards together. I would play with my toys or read. Radio did not isolate families. It was, and is, a shared, not solitary, experience.

My radio days are alive now only in memory. Time moves on, we are told. Things change. That may be so . . . but not always for the better.

Malden Man

My father loved Malden. It was unequivocal, unflagging and blind love. It had nothing to do with fairness or balance, if it was about Malden, it was good. Period.

His parents, exiles from Czarist Russia, brought him to a little two-family house on Harrison Street, right off Eastern Avenue and next to the railroad tracks, when he was a kid of six.

Malden was never out of his heart from that day in 1910 until his death 64 years later. He was, proudly, an American, a Maldonian and a Democrat. When the born-in America generation began to make a few dollars, the out-migration from Malden began: Lynn, Peabody, Swampscott, right up the North Shore of Massachusetts, and later westward toward the Berkshires. About this development he would say, with more than a touch of irony in his voice: "As soon as these guys get $200 in the bank, they become Republicans and leave Malden."

Over the years, relatives and friends would chide him for his allegiance to Malden. "What's holding you here?" they would ask. "How can you compare Malden with Westwood or Peabody?" He would smile, benignly, at this poor soul who, in his estimation, had sold his birthright for a split-level ranch house in some "foreign" town. "This is where I belong," he would answer.

Malden held his memories of the early days in the Daniels School, and of that sunny day in the school yard, when at age 12, he first set eyes on Sophia, the doe-eyed daughter of Dutch immigrants—but more important, now a Malden girl. Thirteen years later, he would marry Sophia, and settle down in a flat just around the corner from his childhood home.

There were other memories, too; some bright, some sad.

- Of his bar mitzvah in the old Beth Israel Synagogue, at the corner of Eastern Avenue and Bryant Street, under the tutelage of the master Rabbi, Ber Borukoff who would later officiate at his wedding;

- Of having to quit school after the eighth grade to help support the family by working in a factory;

- Of the night his father, a disciplinarian in the old European tradition, beat him and locked him out of the house for being late, and of his resolve right then to go it on his own.

He would have to leave Malden now. At the age of 14, carrying a birth certificate from an uncle several years his senior, he set out with a friend on a beat-up motorcycle. They traveled from one ocean to the other, over dirt roads and primitive highways, landing many weeks later in San Diego, California, where they promptly joined the Navy.

World War I was still raging and, before his 15th birthday, he saw action aboard a battleship off the French coast. For the next seven years he remained a sailor (except for the year he spent in a missionary school in China when the Navy discovered he was underage).

After the service years, he tried his luck at running a garage in Birmingham, Alabama. But, Sophia and Malden beckoned, and sometime late in 1928, he came back home.

And for the next 50 years, Malden was his only home. When finally he could afford a down payment, he bought a house—not in some "foreign" town, but right up on Belmont Hill. In other words, the progression was always upward, but not outward. His thinking about where a person should live was circumscribed by the borders of Malden.

He remained always a booster for Malden, and demonstrated his affection by many acts of community service, some public but quite a few that remained anonymous. Whether as commander of the Jewish War Veterans, as an active member of the American Legion, or as a leader in the gala observance of Malden's 150th birthday, for him it was happening in Malden. And it wasn't just some quirky habit that his last act every weeknight was to read the Malden News, every word of it from front to back. It was more like an act of faith.

He completed his journey through life on a blizzard-driven January morning in 1978 at the Malden Hospital. He would have asked for no finer epitaph than this:

"Harry Abelson. He lived in Malden."

A Visit to My Father's Grave

The cemetery where my father is buried is not in some bucolic setting, surrounded by trees beside a quiet brook. It sits between an ugly strip shopping mall and a gaudy real estate company. It is fronted by busy Route 28 in North Reading, Massachusetts. The roar of cars and trucks is endless.

It had been several years since I had made a pilgrimage to my dad's grave, even though I had passed by a few times. This time I stopped. Dina remembered the grave was away back near the fence, and called "Here it is. Here it is."

I joined her at the triple headstone which still had blank sheets of granite waiting for the names of my mother and brother. It said: "Harry A. Abelson. Loving husband, father and grandfather. 1904-1978."

A shudder ran through me as I reached out and touched the stone, warmed by the summer sun. I remembered a man barely educated, who sought his entire life to improve himself, who worked hard to take care of his family. But also a man who had never professed, out loud, his love for me, or anyone else. With his death went any chance, it seemed, to ever work out my unresolved feelings about him.

My father appeared to me, in my youth, to be unshakable. So it was both sobering and frightening to witness the vulnerability of so strong and self-contained a man.

The first time occurred in my teens after my father's father, a recent widower, came to live in our house. Always a difficult man, my grandfather became more and more irrational and demanding as time passed. It is clear, in retrospect, that he suffered from Alzheimer's disease.

One day, as my grandfather was especially trying, complaining and muttering oaths at my mother, my father just came apart. In tears, he pleaded and screamed: "Pa, pa, for God's sake, stop the craziness. Let us live. Let us live." I was confused and frightened. Never again would I feel as safe and protected.

The second, and last, time my dad's human frailty became apparent was many years later, as he lay dying from lung cancer. He seemed so small and vulnerable there in a hospital bed. I spent those last six weeks visiting my father nearly every day and, being the night person in the family, staying alone with him until late in the evening.

He was unable to sleep much, but in all the hours we two spent together, he said not a word about his impending death. He imparted no last words, nor did we exchange any words of love or affection. Even at the last.

On New Year's Eve, my father called and asked me to join him for the hospital's celebration. When I got there, he seemed more lively and in less pain. He even ate a few shrimp and flirted with a nurse in a party hat. I stayed until daylight, as I sensed he wanted me to. But we said little to each other.

Harry Abelson died 18 days later. He was buried during a lull in the raging blizzard of 1978. How appropriate. Now, on a blazing hot summer day 17 years later, I pick up a pebble from the ground and, as is the Jewish custom, place it atop my father's gravestone.

As I turn to leave, I whisper through my tears: "Damn it, daddy. I love you."

"Where Have You Gone, Joe DiMaggio?"

I could smell the sausages frying from the parking lot half a mile away from Fenway Park. At only $10, the dusty lot was a bargain, said my son David, whose guest I was for a twi-night doubleheader between the Red Sox and the Baltimore Orioles. It was my first Fenway outing in years.

As we made our way to our seats, about 25 rows high in the grandstand just up from the batter's box along the first-base line, I was already being pitched back in time. By the second game, I was again the 12-year-old kid munching on a 10-cent hot dog, dripping mustard all over my shorts and joining the crowd in singing at the top of my lungs (to the tune of "Oh, Tannenbaum"):

"He's better than his brother Joe . . . Domenic DiMaggio . . ."

Dom was the quiet and dependable DiMaggio brother, ranging the outfield for the Sox, hitting well up in the .300s and exuding the modesty and quiet leadership we see exhibited by Cal Ripken. When Joe DiMaggio and the Yankees came to Bean Town, it was always a thrill to see the brothers go against each other.

But the real big deal, of course, was Joltin' Joe against the Splendid Splinter, Ted Williams, whose .406 batting average in 1941 has been unmatched since.

It was a grand exhibition in differences between two giants, two geniuses in their field, two men—rightly or wrongly—perceived very differently by the fans. Joe would come loping onto the field, all smiles and teeth, responding to the screaming kids like me (I was a secret Yankee fan for awhile), and even tipping his cap. He seemed good-natured even while being part of a killer Yankee lineup that too often decimated the BoSox. And when he hit a four-bagger, he would swing that bat around in a mighty arc that made you know in advance what was in the making.

With Williams, it was more like a chess champ coming to the board—the brains in motion, off on another plane, almost unaware of the fans shouting, of his long legs carrying him with such grace. And he looked so much younger than Joe. (Maybe he was; I don't know their comparative ages.) He earned another, less used nickname, The Kid.

In his concentration, that eye-to-hand coordination that Ph.D. theses have been written about, he didn't seem to have the time or awareness for niceties like smiling and removing his cap. And, one guesses, he wondered why he should have to tap-dance for the fans in addition to the wondrous way he did his job.

But, listen, all was forgiven when he came to bat. There may have been nine opposing team members to this one Red Sox, but with the club in William's hand, it was all even. He was quiet in the batter's box. He would eye the pitcher like a laser beam. It was said he could count the stitches on the ball as it sped toward him.

Then, unlike DiMaggio's round-house swing, you would hear a cra-a-a-ck, almost missing the quick movement of the bat, and it was all over. When Williams was at bat, there was little the defense could do. Swinging around the field in the Williams Shift didn't work. Strategy conferences on the mound between pitcher and catcher were no good. Often, trying to catch the corners, the pitchers would give up a base on balls. Ted was not always happy when he wasn't given anything half-good to swing at.

I was brought back to real time when Mo Vaughn, still a Red Sox that year, hitting one of his 6-for-7 for the day, belted one outta there. Neither of his two homers had anything to apologize for. Mo reminded me of an earlier Sox first baseman, Rudy York. York, a huge man of American Indian heritage, nearly filled up the batter's box with his bulk, leaving little room for the pitcher to maneuver. But, lord, was he slow. The joke was when he belted one way out into Fenway's center-field triangle, it would be an inside-the-park single.

What I missed this trip was the pepper, the nervous movement in the infield, especially around second base, and the taunting of the batter, encouragement of the pitcher. These guys seemed to be out there counting their commercial money and waiting for a ball to come to them.

In my early days, the Sox had one of the truly great combos with Bobby Doerr at second and Johnny Pesky at shortstop. They were opposites in personality—Doerr the quiet gentlemanly and brainy player, Pesky noisy and nervous, moving in all directions at once. But somehow their minds were connected, each knowing the other's next step without looking.

This was the first time I had seen Cal Ripken, and his quiet and unassuming manner while performing baseball magic reminded me, in a way, of the great Detroit Tigers slugger, Hank Greenberg. One day my friend Richie and I pushed our way up to the visitors' dugout as Greenberg was heading for the on deck circle. "Hank, Hank," we shouted out. He stopped, turned and waved at two 12-year-olds who had a story they could tell more than half a century later.

Echoes. And memories.

As darkness fell, and lights illuminated the field of dreams, my mind wandered back again as I heard the voice of the great Sox radio announcer, Jim Britt, intoning his favorite line when there was a full count on a batter. It resonated with me, an aging guy who still has some of the boy in him: "It's three and two—the big one due."

Goodbye Old House

A fading photograph, lined with jagged cracks testifying to the near century since it was taken, shows my mother at age 6, sitting on her front steps with her younger brother and sister. I found it at the bottom of an old cigar box filled with moments in time from the lives of my parents and their families.

As I sat alone in the dead silence of the two-family house I lived in from age 14 until I left home eight years later, it occurred to me that home is not only where the heart is, but also where memories reside. When my father died some two decades before, I insisted that my mother sell the old house and move closer to us. She looked me straight in the eye and said: "I'm staying here, where my memories are."

Now I was faced with the responsibility—and the sadness—of selling the house my parents had purchased a half century earlier. It was the first and only house my parents ever owned; they never had much money, and the $7,000 cost of the house in 1945 was a huge expenditure for them.

I felt almost like an intruder, sifting through their personal effects. There was a bundle of love letters, tied by a crumbling ribbon, written by Harry to Sophia in the early 1920s. My dad was in the middle of his eight-year hitch in the Navy, and the envelopes bore postmarks from all over the world. It's difficult to attribute the passion and tenderness in those letters to the guy I called daddy, and who never showed much affection to my mother in public.

Then I came upon my mother's jewelry—not the diamonds Dad gave her in the latter years, when he was doing better, but the costume jewelry, the faux stones and colorful enamels that mirrored her life in the '30s. And there were the hand-me-downs, the few possessions their parents carried across the Atlantic in their emigrations. There were little holiday wine glasses, a chipped serving platter, a set of tiny teaspoons with windmills on them.

But it was the photos, hundreds of them tracing three generations, that sent my mind reeling back in time.

There was my dad in his Navy blues sitting atop a camel with the pyramids in the background; swigging a beer with a buddy on the Riviera; with his arm around a pretty young thing in a Parisian sidewalk café. Later, a snap of him in his American Legion uniform, marching down Pleasant Street in Malden, Massachusetts. And dad all spiffed up in a gleaming white, double-breasted suit, leaning jauntily on a Malacca cane.

Then I came upon a stunning picture of my mother, from the 1920s, dressed as a flapper; wearing a skin-tight sheath dress and cloche hat covering her bobbed hair; flashing a coquettish smile. Had my quiet old housekeeper of a mom been, in her youth, a swinger? Does she think about those times, dancing the night away at a Harvard fraternity party, as she sits in her wheelchair in her room at the nursing home? I found myself crying softly for the lost youths of Harry and Sophia.

It seemed impossible to choose what to keep and what to throw out from these precious belongings representing more than a century in the life of my family. I wandered into my old bedroom, still holding mementos from my childhood, and realized that, for the first time in all my 60-plus years, I would be without a bedroom in my parents' house.

As I packed the pictures into boxes, I noticed something different about the house. It was quiet. For the first time in five decades, it was quiet, and unlived in.

Suddenly I was roused from my reverie by a ringing telephone. It was my wife calling from the house, 70 miles away, that we have shared for some 30 years.

It was time to leave. For the first time there was no one to say goodbye to in the old house. But as I left, I said goodbye anyway, and—for the last time—pulled the door shut.

Being and Doing Jewish

Marrying into Memory

I t is difficult to remember, these nearly 50 years later, whether it was viewing a movie called "The Juggler" or seeing for the first time the fading, blue tattoo. It is important because it has to do with the first time I made the connection between myself-both as a Jew and a human being—and the reality of the Holocaust.

I was a 23-year-old, non-practicing Jew from an Orthodox family settled for a generation in a working-class community outside of Boston. I had come north to Concord, New Hampshire, on a work assignment. Dina, a Jew from Poland whose family was engulfed in the Holocaust and who herself was a survivor of Auschwitz, had recently left New York to care for her father, also a survivor, who was employed as a master tanner in Concord. We were introduced on a blind date and within a week I had proposed. Three months later we were engaged and six months after that there was a gala wedding.

In retrospect I can say with honesty, that my initial feelings toward Dina were unrelated to her wartime experiences. There I was, a young Jewish American, a practicing journalist, and yet I felt no connection with and had no meaningful knowledge about those years of horror, years through which I also had lived. In September of 1939, as the Nazi machine pushed into Poland, I was playing the play of an eight-and-a-half year old, toting my toy gun to kill all the bad guys. On VE Day, I was an adolescent who joined with the neighbors in singing patriotic songs and enjoying a picnic. Nothing said or felt about them, our Jews in darkness. At least not by me.

I had celebrated my bar mitzvah more than a year earlier. What were they doing, I wonder now, my wife and family-to-be, on that unseasonably warm Shabbat in March of 1944? I was standing, frightened and confused, on the bimah in an old Orthodox synagogue, chanting my Torah portion and reciting from rote a speech written by my rabbi. It was an old standard, thanking my parents for bringing me up as a Jew, and detailing Jacob's wrestling bout with the angel. But nothing about them, our Jews in darkness. Not a word or a murmur. At least not from me.

When Shabbat ended, we gathered for a party. It was a gay evening with an overflow of kosher food and drink. All of my relatives, including the ones with the accents—my zayde and his brothers and sisters who had escaped the oppressive anti-Semitism of Eastern Europe— were there. All of our neighbors and my father's business associates, nearly all Christian, were there. We danced and we sang, Yiddish songs with verse upon verse, many of them improvised to fit the occasion. My father stood on a table leading all the rest: "Bim, bom, bim-bim-bim, bom . . ." But still, nothing about them, our Jews in darkness. Not a thought. At least not from me.

For me, the war was air raid drills, rationing and war movies on Saturday afternoon. What did I know of them? I knew nothing. How conscious was I of the starvation, the torture, the gassing, the incineration? I was not conscious of it at all. How many prayers did I speak on their behalf? None.

In the after-war years of 1946 to 1949, those who had lived so long with death were trying to cope again with life, no homes to return to, most of their families wiped out, moving from concentration camp to displaced person camp. In those same years, I was in high school preparing for my future. I was the accordionist for the German Honor Society, playing and singing the old beer hall songs with great gusto. As to our Jews of darkness, now called Survivors, I still gave no thought.

Yet, just five year later I was walking into a theater in Concord, New Hampshire, on my third date with a young woman who had been through the worst of it, from Auschwitz and back. The film we watched unfolded the experiences of a Holocaust survivor, a juggler by profession, as he made his way through a maze of DP camps, and his heroic but unsuccessful attempts to reach Israel. At some point in the movie, I began to feel uneasy, and I thought: "My God, what have I done?" How could I be so unfeeling as to bring this young woman to such a film? I asked her if she wished to leave; she said that she would stay. Not knowing what to say, I reached out and our hands remained locked together through the rest of the film. Afterward, as we walked back to her apartment, conversation was strained. Years passed before we were able to discuss that evening.

With the tattoo, it happened suddenly. One evening, at dinner at her home, Dina removed the jacket of her suit, and I saw it there, imprinted on the inside of her forearm: the Auschwitz A followed by several identification numerals. I was not unaware of this Nazi practice, but seeing the tattoo for the first time, and on the arm of this graceful woman whom I already had come to love, unleashed my anger. For the first time in my life, I wanted to kill. I wanted to feel myself killing Nazis. But it was not possible for such feelings to be sustained for long in that home. Both Dina and her father, Israel, seemed incapable of hatred; bitterness was a stranger in their home. This confused me.

Before long, I was a nightly addition to their dinner table and after-meal discussion. Israel had determined that I was "a nice boy" who was away from home and who needed to be fed and otherwise nurtured. This new aspect of family life, shared with these two lovely people, made me want to learn more about the Holocaust from the lips of the survivors. But a contradiction existed: the more conscious and curious I became, the more sensitive I was about not dredging up the terrible memories for Dina and her father. Only with time would I learn the proper balance between the two tendencies.

The mother, the oldest son and the youngest daughter, Bella, had been murdered. The father and his six remaining children had, miraculously, survived the death camps. Five of the children already were married to other survivors at the time of my marriage to Dina. I was the first outsider in the family, and despite the warm flow of affection I received from the beginning, I was quite aware of the difference.

First there was language. When the family gathered, depending upon who was speaking to whom, I heard Polish, Yiddish and German, with sprinklings of Swedish and French. But they often used English, as well—my feelings of being an outsider in my new family were due not only to different languages. No, the reason was that these people and I were different. Their experiences had taken them beyond my ability to understand, beyond even my ability to imagine. Their courage, their endurance, their will to live had been tested far beyond anything I could comprehend. I knew that there was a part of Dina's experience that always would be separate from our life together, no matter how deep our love or close our friendship. Something removed, never to be shared.

Back then, in those first days, I was far from comfortable. I was ashamed of how little I knew of the times and events through which this family had lived. Quickly, I came to love them, and they reciprocated. But I worried: what would they think if they discovered how uninformed I was? Fortunately for me, they were wise enough to sense my feelings. Piece by piece, slowly at first, they began to tell me the story. My shame gave way to a new tangle of emotions. I didn't want to hear the stories, yet I knew that I had to listen. I must listen.

While the entire family has helped with my education, the oldest brother, Alter, has been my mentor. He has held back nothing. For more than 45 years he has been telling me the story, and the end still is not in sight. How many nights have we sat up together until dawn, while the family slept? He tells me how it was and how it felt, recalling the most minute details. I listen, in a semi-trance, uttering not a sound. As the hours pass, his voice smoothes out, softens. One tale reminds him of another, some horrible, others lighter. Black beads of inhuman atrocity strung between little jewels of humor. At first, humor seemed out of place, irreverent, in the Holocaust. I have come to understand that humor holds a place of honor in the worst of Jewish experience.

Now, I am actually able to join in the laughter. It is as close as I have been able to get, perhaps as close as I ever will get. It is I, the outsider, who asks questions, presses for details, laughs at incidents from a time of hell—almost as if I had been one of them.

Then it strikes me. Were we not all slaves in Egypt? Am I not a Jew, even as they are Jews? Perhaps I never can be one of them, but I know that always I have been one *with* them.

Bella's Encounter with God*

Hello, my name is Bella. I am eleven years old; I will always be eleven years old. But despite the fact that I am not alive, I am not yet at rest.

When I first came to God, I asked him to be united again with my Momma, my brother, Moniek, and my Grandpa, the Rabbi. But God said I could not rest with them until I answered a question for him. Can you imagine God asking a child to answer a question for him? I was really scared.

God said not to be afraid because, after all, how frightening and powerful could He be if He had to ask me to answer a question? He said if I didn't know the answer myself, I would have to learn it from the living people. So for nearly 50 years, I have been traveling the earth asking God's question, but getting no answer. Finally, I decided to come to this place where Dina, my red-haired sister, lives; I ask you to help me find an answer for God so I can be with my Momma again.

Maybe it would help if you knew about me. I was born in the Polish city of Radom some 70 years ago. It was a community of 100,000 people, with 30,000 of us Jews. Jews had lived in Radom for a very long time. We were a happy family, as happy as anybody can be when they are surrounded by people, most of whom hate them.

My Daddy owned a tannery and my Momma took care of me and my three sisters and four brothers. No one ever had better parents and family. We lived in a nice house, and rode around in a droschke, what you would call a horse and buggy. We had good times together, and laughed and played a lot.

I had wonderful grandparents, but I especially remember Grandpa Elias, the Rabbi. He had a thick beard and always wore a long, black coat. His eyes were kind, but altogether, he was scary to a little girl. Until I met the real one, I had thought maybe Grandpa Elias was God.

---

*Bella, the youngest sister of Dina Abelson, the author's wife, was murdered at Auschwitz.

In the fall of 1939, the bombings started. We would have to run down to our cellar, a cold and damp place where we kept the vegetables. Then one day, the Germans came and took away our house and herded us into a ghetto. I don't remember much about what followed, except that, one by one, all the men, including my daddy and my brothers, were taken away. Then one day they came for us.

We went on a train. There were no windows and no seats. Oh, it was so hot, and we were all squashed together, and there was no bathroom, and there was no food, and there was no water.

When we got off the cattle-cars, there were a lot of men in uniforms screaming at us and hitting some of the old people because they were too slow.

I was so frightened I was shaking. Suddenly, the SS officer in charge asked me how old I was. When I told, the man—his name was Dr. Mengele—moved his thumb in one direction, and I was pushed away from my sisters and Momma. Momma walked right up to the man and begged him to let her go with me. And he did.

Now we were standing in a long line in front of a big building; the soldiers told us we were going to take a shower. The next thing I knew, I was standing in front of God, and I was crying for my Momma. Then I noticed that God was crying too.

He said, "Bella, before I take you to your Momma, you must find for me the answer to a question." I said, "But I thought You knew everything."

"From the beginning of time," He said, "always I have known the answers—until now. Bella, go to the people; find the answer."

"What is the question you don't know the answer to, God?"

"The question, Bella, is Why?"

What is it to be a Jew?

What is it to be a Jew, a Jew is asked. It is asked by those who love him; it asked by those who despise him. It is asked by the friend; it is asked by the stranger. And, not infrequently, it is asked by the Jew to him or herself. Is it a religion or a race or a nationality, or what, I have been asked. Over time, it has been each and every one of these, I have answered, and to those who have followed its light, it has been a way of life. It has been a source of knowledge and joy, and it has been a cause for torture and death.

Let me tell you what else it is to be a Jew. It is to be self-conscious. It is to be in a nearly constant state of forgiveness. It is to be ambivalent, to be suspicious and watchful. It is to be proud of surviving and sick and tired of being a survivor. It is to be compassionate and contributing to society and wondering why you are hated for it. It is even thinking what it would be like to be a Christian, how it would feel to be in the majority, how it would seem to live without being reviled, murdered or accused of deicide.

About being self-conscious: years ago, a business group was meeting with a CPA we were considering hiring. Things were going well until the accountant was talking about a case of arson and referred to it as "Jewish lightning." Of the four potential clients, two of us were Jewish and a third was part Jewish. Many years before, I had felt sorry for a lonely young woman who had moved up from the South to a job where I worked in Boston, and asked her out to dinner. During the meal, she turned to me and said: "You know, there's only one thing ah hate worse than a niggah and that's a Jew." How many times over the years has someone told me with pride how he "Jewed down" some merchant? And all the references to New York "kikes" and Jewish American princesses—always quick to add "of course, you're not like them." Without reference to how I respond, usually with vehemence, think about a life spent having to wonder when the next person you like is going to force you to make a choice.

About forgiving: Christians, in general, expect Jews to forgive. It is, after all, an important part of what they believe (and not an inconsequential part of what Jews practice). I, and most of my co-religionists, have done a pretty good job, I believe, of forgiving. We have been less successful with the other half of the forgiveness precept—namely, living. One of the problems I perceive is a matter of time. Given the Biblical timeline of three score and ten, there hardly would be the opportunity to forgive everyone. Let's see, forgive the Pharaohs. Forgive the Romans. Forgive Herod and Haman. Forgive the destruction of the First Temple; forgive the destruction of the Second Temple. Forgive the expulsion from the homeland the first time, and all the subsequent times (including present-day objectives of some). Forgive the 14th Century slaughter of Jews accused of causing the Plague. Forgive the Inquisition. Forgive the expulsion from Spain and its attendant cruelties. Forgive the pogroms in the pale of settlement in Russia; forgive the endless suffering imposed by the church and state and army and later by the Communists. Forgive the writers of the Protocols of the Elders of Zion.

And forgive the oppressors of Alfred Dreyfus and all the others who have turned the patriotism of those Jews who loved the nations in which they lived, into ashes. Forgive Martin Luther for calling the Jews "disgusting vermin" and recommending their synagogues be burned and all their home destroyed. Forgive Pope Pius XII for his silence and that of most of the churches during the Holocaust. Forgive the Poles and the French for the relish they took in pointing out Jews to the Nazis. Forgive the Ukrainians and the Croatians for treating the Jews with such cruelty that even their German overlords were repelled. Forgive the American government for turning away a shipload of Jews who were forced to return to Europe and their death; and forgive repressive immigration laws that kept Jews from these shores. Forgive Franklin D. Roosevelt and his cohorts for refusing to bomb the rail lines into Auschwitz and the crematoria and gas chambers inside that hell.

Forgive those world powers who opposed creation of Israel as a safe haven for the survivors of the Holocaust. Forgive the Arab states, 50 million strong, who attacked Israel the day after its official creation. Forgive Louis Farrakhan, who called Judaism a "gutter religion." Forgive Ronald Reagan for his trip to Bitburg to honor, among others, the graves of SS murderers. Forgive Patrick Buchanan who said Hitler was an "individual of great courage" and that "half the survivors' testimonies at Yad Vashem are unreliable." And forgive those who are teaching at American colleges that the Holocaust was exaggerated or never happened. And forgive President Tudjman of Croatia for writing "A Jew is still a Jew . . . even in the camps they retained their . . . selfishness, perfidy, meanness, slyness and treacherousness."

Forgive those kids who used to beat me up on my way to Hebrew school. Forgive those German soldiers who shot at my wife, and the Auschwitz guards who turned her childhood into a lifelong nightmare. Forgive Dr. Mengele who sent her mother and little sister to the gas chamber. Forgive those anti-Semites at the Small Business Administration in Boston who wouldn't stay in the same room with me and forced me out of my job. Forgive those staff people at the Fernald School for the retarded who called my afflicted brother "dirty fucking Jew."

Forgive them, one and all, and move on, we are counseled. All right, but move on to what? The resurgence of Nazism across Western Europe, especially in Germany. Former SS men are welcomed to one community to celebrate Hitler's birthday. Skinheads, mouthing the Nazi line, march in torchlight parades. In France, the ultra right becomes more vocal and numerous. In Poland, where there remain few Jews, Jews still are blamed for the nation's woes. In Russia, there has been a rebirth of the Cossacks, those erstwhile defenders of the tsar and tormentors of the Jews; some say their number is well over a million. In this country, anti-Semitic incidents reached record highs in recent years; and for the first time, attacks on people outnumbered attacks on Jewish owned property, cemeteries and synagogues.

Those things, and more, explain the suspicion and watchfulness of the Jews. But to be a Jew also means, in the darkest moments, to have hope. My brother-in-law, Al, teaching Latin to my wife in Poland while the bombs fell. The prayer services at Auschwitz. The poems written and pictures painted under the noses of the German guards. The uprising in the Warsaw ghetto. The miracle of the survivors rebuilding their lives and bringing children into a world that stood silent while 1.5 million Jewish children were exterminated.

In the final analysis, to be a Jew is to be a human being and to say to you, our Christian brothers and sisters: as you would have us treat you, in that way treat us.

"Schindler's List"—
A Minority View

"Schindler's List," Steven Spielberg's film that has injected the Holocaust story into the popular culture, is another episode in depicting Jews as passive victims.

Through the centuries, Jews have been stereotyped as troublemakers, calculating money-grubbers, cowards who run rather than stand and fight. Their stories often have been told second-hand, twisted, by non-Jews, from William Shakespeare's insidious portrayal of the Merchant of Venice to William Styron's lazily researched Sophie's Choice.

And even when Jews are depicted as muddling through a bad time, frequently it is non-Jews who provide the stiff upper lip, and rescue them. The most famous Holocaust story to make its way into the popular culture is The Diary of a Young Girl by Anne Frank. It is the tale of one hapless Jewish family hidden away by a courageous and caring gentile family. Of course, Anne and her family were also courageous, but by circumstance were dependent for their very existence on their non-Jewish benefactors.

The acclaimed television drama some years ago, Holocaust, also made its way into the public consciousness. It was told in significant measure through the eyes of a Nazi SS officer, who showed flashes of compassion toward a German-Jewish family, stripped of its wealth and self-assurance.

Then came Schindler's List. For most of the millions who usually rush to a Spielberg block-buster, this movie will become the paradigm for the Holocaust. Long after its first run in movie houses in all parts of the globe, it will continue to be shown in schools, churches and synagogues, accompanied often by lectures from learned people discussing the heroism and motivations of a Nazi.

Oskar Schindler is a German industrialist who fattens his coffers by offering bribes to Nazi officials and making liberal use of Jewish labor. At some point, Schindler "sees the light" through some kind of epiphany. He will draw up a salvation list. He will save Jews. And he does manage to save over a thousand of these "wretches."

So let's give Schindler the benefit of the doubt. Let's say it was the revelation and guilt that moved him. Let's say he emerged finally as a genuine hero, despite the doubts expressed even by his widow as to his motivation. After all, as Jews are taught, it is the act that counts.

But the question remains: Why has Spielberg chosen to tell the story of the Holocaust through the eyes of a non-Jew, a member of the Nazi party dedicated to murdering every Jew in the world? Since there is little chance that I will have the opportunity to ask him personally, I must conjecture. Spielberg might respond: "I can't tell just any story. It must be dramatic. It must be able to capture the interest of the mass of moviegoers."

All right, I reply. You want drama? Jewish youngsters with a handful of outdated weapons stand off Nazi battalions for more than six weeks in the Warsaw Ghetto, freely choosing death over capture. Jewish women, forced to work in a munitions factory for the Germans, smuggle explosives into the death camp at Auschwitz, so their comrades can blow up the crematoria where they collect the bones and ashes of the dead. The women are hanged. My mother-in-law, whom I never knew, chooses to accompany her doomed youngest daughter into the gas chamber, so the little girl will not be afraid.

Jewish freedom fighters, many of them teenage boys and girls, strike out at the Nazis from the forests and mountains in the occupied countries. Torahs are smuggled into concentration camps; religious services are held. Plays are written and performed. My sister-in-law's father, himself frail and near death from starvation, gives away a piece of bread to a fellow prisoner.

Why not a seminal film about a day in the life of a death camp prisoner? Is there a more dramatic or heroic human act than conjuring up hope in a place of no hope, and each day choosing life in a heartless place of death? Is there a more courageous story to be told than that of my wife's journey from a happy middle-class childhood to ghetto to Auschwitz to survival to renewal? I think not.

Or, as we passed the 50th anniversary of their presence among us, why not tell the story of Jewish survivors in the United States and Canada? This epic of courage and rebirth is both startling and uplifting. There is real drama in this story of human transcendence.

One of the finest films of the American experience in World War II was The Best Years Of Our Lives. It told not the gory tale of battle-front engagements, but rather the bittersweet story of three servicemen and the difficulty of their post-war adjustments when they returned home to the states and their families. It was not told through the eyes of some courageous Europeans who sheltered and saved American servicemen, although these things certainly occurred. It was told, as well it should have been, through the eyes of the Americans themselves.

Don't get me wrong. I have the highest admiration for each and every act of courage in the face of certain death performed by righteous Gentiles to save Jews. They have earned a place among our greatest heroes. Their stories must be kept alive.

But is it not time, at long last, for a block-buster film to bring into the popular culture the story of the Holocaust through the heroic lives and brave acts of the people who went through it? Is it not time to make the world aware of Jewish resistance and of Jewish refusal to be obliterated in the midst of a genocide that was all but ignored by the so-called civilized nations and their people?

Steven Spielberg is among the few with the money, the power and the talent who could have told this story, a Jewish story. He chose otherwise. He was finally vindicated as a filmmaker this year when "Schindler's List" won him an armful of Academy Awards. Hopefully, this success will prompt Spielberg one day to produce a movie about Jewish heroism and resistance during the Holocaust.

Where Was Man?

How could God let Auschwitz happen? Where was God at Masada, at the pogroms, during the Inquisition, the Spanish expulsion? Why didn't he strike down Martin Luther when he called Jews "disgusting vermin" and exhorted Christians to burn Jews' homes and synagogues? Or when Louis Farrakhan said we Jews practice a "gutter religion"? (Excuse me, he now says he only called it a "dirty religion.")

Where was God when some citizens spray-painted swastikas and the words "Jews drink blood," on our newly re-built Temple Beth Jacob? Or when 100 Jewish gravestones were overturned in Massachusetts? And, dare I ask, where was the God of Israel when my wife's mother and little sister, Bella, walked naked into the gas chamber at Auschwitz?

And one can ask, on behalf of others, where are You, God, as the young girls in Bosnia are being raped and then having their severed heads handed to their mothers? And where were you in the killing fields of Cambodia? And so many other places.

Let me pose some possible answers:

Maybe there is no God, as many millions have believed—including me, on and off during my life. Or maybe God is a limited God as Rabbi Harold Kushner has posited, and has neither the time, the inclination nor the power to handle all this trouble. Perhaps God is a vengeful Lord, as the fringe groups in many religions, including mine, believe.

Or it could be that when Adam and Eve opted in favor of the tree of knowledge, God said "Okay, I'm letting you in on the big secret, and giving you free will. But then I'm retiring. Oh, I'll hand out a set of rules (the Torah) down the line, but essentially you're on your own."

Let me tell you what I'm coming to believe, more and more, as the hair gets grayer and the knees get weaker: God is in large measure a reflection of how people treat each other . . . a reflection of the compassion—or lack of it—that God commanded us to exercise. Maybe God has kept the promise; it is we who have broken it. Maybe God is there when needed, it is *we* who are absent.

I sometimes think God already has sent the Messiah. What if the Messiah has already been here a hundred times, a thousand times, and we have failed to recognize it? Maybe the Messiah is that dirty, mentally disturbed homeless person we turn away from. Or the poor, single mother we brand a "welfare queen" because she cheats so she can get a little food for her kids and also keep them warm in the winter. It could be the black person we denigrate as a "shwartze," or the fellow Jew we don't like and spread malicious gossip about.

We are engulfed in our own narcissism, our hubris, our stiff-necked belief that we are living just lives, when we are really only living safe and comfortable lives. We do not steal for our kids because we do not have to. We do not scream in the streets, or act out, or have fist fights, because we can hire lawyers and doctors and psychologists. And the police respect us. When was the last time we looked at a Down syndrome youngster, or the parents who have just buried a child and said: "There but for the grace of God go I"?

Speaking as a parent who has buried a child and the brother of a man who lived for 30 years in a state institution, and the husband of a woman who lived inside the gates of hell at Auschwitz, I think about it a lot.

My mother, who had absolutely no Jewish education or upbringing, was Jewish in her heart. It was she who made sure my Hebrew homework was done. It was she who gave over her life to my brother. It was she who taught me the important lessons. For instance, there was only one family of black people in our neighborhood, maybe in the whole city. Their name was Sparrow. My mother used to invite Mrs. Sparrow over for tea in the afternoon, and they would chat and laugh together about running a household where money was scarce. Later, I asked my mother patronizingly if she had consciously reached out because the woman was black. "I invited her because she is a nice lady." Sophia did not stand idly by.

And so the Jewish concept of Tikkun Olam, the repair of the world, was early instilled into me. But it has only been in recent years, that I have hooked up the repair of the world with a command to me as a Jew. It has been a revelation, and in some ways, a gift, that it has come to me late in life. Because it has been a conscious choice.

Albert Einstein was asked by a non-Jewish colleague after the outbreak of Fascism, "Now, aren't you sorry you were born a Jew?" Einstein replied: "Yes, I'm sorry I was born a Jew. I wish I had come to Judaism not by the accident of birth, but after ascertaining its worth."

When faced with the command to act, some ask what one person can do alone.

Several years ago, our local newspaper ran a series of articles on my wife's life and wartime experiences. In an editorial following the series, the editor wrote: "It was her duty to tell the story; ours is to listen, to feel compassion and to overcome the tendency to remain silent in the face of evil."

People have listened, and they certainly have shown compassion for suffering. The hard part for us all is overcoming silence in the face of evil. In Judaism, it is said that the act is everything. It is not enough to show compassion for suffering. Each of us must act.

When Elie Weisel, the Holocaust survivor and Nobel Peace laureate, was asked why he went to Bosnia, why he took the risk of visiting the concentration camps holding Croats and Muslims, who have been enemies of the Jews, he replied: "I am compelled to be here. Where there is injustice and suffering, I have no choice but to go."

We here do not have to travel to Bosnia to act. We must recognize as evil, and act against, any system that despises the poor; that turns its eyes away from mentally ill homeless; that allows children to go hungry; that sanctions the closing of libraries; that ignores education; that allows the elderly to be thrown out of their homes; that withholds medical care from the bottom rung of society; that hardens its heart against the weak, the humble, the lost.

Does religion serve *any* purpose at all if it does not serve these purposes? If it does not speak out, if it does not act? The Talmud says "The pious promise little, but perform much." And it teaches further that while we are not expected to complete the difficult tasks before us, we are required to start them.

We have an opportunity, an opportunity to alleviate the suffering of our fellow humans who pass all too often unnoticed among us. The homeless. The old. The hungry. The mentally ill and the physically impaired. The people who try, and just cannot seem to make it. And the ones who do not even try, because they do not know how. They, too, are survivors. Each of them.

The ancient Greek statesman, Pericles, said: "We regard the individual who takes no part in civic affairs as useless." We cannot afford to be useless. The day is short and the task is mighty. When will we start?

True Love, Yiddish Style

When I was a child of six or seven, my most vibrant Jewish experience occurred every Sunday morning, when I accompanied my father on his weekly visit to his parents. Bobe and Zeyde owned a broken-down, two-family house that sat between a working class bar and grill, and the Boston & Maine Railroad tracks along the old Malden Creek.

Inside, the house was a garden of wonderful smells. It seemed that always schmaltz was being rendered into its constituent parts of chicken fat, the cooking liquid of choice for meat dishes, and grivines, those irresistible leftover crunchy bits that were a sensation on a fresh chunk of pumpernickel from Malitsky's Bakery. When I would wander out onto the sun porch to play my little boy's imagination games, I would inhale the pungent smell of horseradish mixed with syrupy sweet redolence of grapes fermenting into wine in a white porcelain jug for the upcoming Passover.

All the while, I knew that my breakfast treat was coming. "Frank," Bobe would say to Zeyde, "go down to Butkavitch and buy a fertl fresh cream cheese and two big bulkes." Every week the same words as she picked out the few pennies for the purchase of the rolls and a quarter-pound of cream cheese from her apron pocket and handed them carefully to my grandfather. On some occasions, she would order him to "nem dos kind mit"—take the child with you. Mumbling Yiddish oaths under his breath, he would take my hand, and we would walk the few blocks to the grocery, just on the periphery of the Jewish ghetto known as Suffolk Square.

And what a store was Butkavitch's! A profusion and a confusion of sights and sounds—and, of course, smells. Sunday morning was always busy, since Jewish stores had been closed from Friday afternoon for the Sabbath. Zeyde would pull me up the three triangular steps and into a babel of Yiddish yelling, pushing, demanding attention, and store clerks serving their friends out of order. Sleeves were rolled up, and hands dashed into barrels full of fat herring and kosher pickles.

Talented index fingers poked into bellies of smoked mackerel and sablefish, testing for freshness. Slabs of sweet creamery butter were scooped out of wooden containers and plopped down onto sheets of oiled paper for wrapping.

Finally, Zeyde got the attention of a clerk, and repeated word-for-word Bobe's instructions. The purchase completed, we would head back to the house. By the time we were in the kitchen, there would be a steaming hot mug of cocoa awaiting me, the first grandson in the family and, therefore, the prince.

Bobe would check the little bag to make sure Frank got it right. Next she would slice open the puffy white rolls and spread each with the cream cheese, and lay them before me.

Then, while the other three would stand by and watch, I would down the entire banquet. No one else ate. Many years later, when I thought about that unusual arrangement, it came to me: My grandparents were dirt poor. Those two rolls and quarter pound of cream cheese were their weekly splurge—it was all they could afford.

So much for a tale of true love.

Peace Needs Hope

It was late March of 1979. There was a touch of Spring in the air. Dina and I sat in the audience on the front lawn outside the White House to witness the signing of the treaty between Israel and Egypt. Within days after the pact, the "history" of the event already was written and spoken by the oracles of our age—the media geniuses and their "highly placed sources"—and already we were in revisionist and post-revisionist periods.

The recent advances of civilization seem to be tied in so many instances to the "know fast—go fast" concept. I, personally, ended a 12-year period of being grounded when I stepped onto the airplane in Boston at 9:15 Monday morning. Twelve hours later, I was back in my living room, having flown to Washington, done a bit of sight-seeing, witnessed the treaty signing, visited a couple of friends, flown back to Boston and driven back to Concord, New Hampshire.

Yes, we were home in plenty of time to hear the State Department and White House correspondents tell us that it was really a very nice ceremony, but that we should not put too much hope in the chances for peace. In the few days after, we all had the opportunity to hear and read much more. Well, I don't mind admitting to being 90 percent of a damned fool. But the other 10 percent made even a simpleton such as me aware of the fact that this treaty was a long way from peace, and even that peace is neither absolute nor static.

I wish to place an indictment not against those who caution us to be aware of human frailty, and the propensity to misdeed and even evil. Rather, I indict those who attempt to murder hope, the kind of hope that both derives from and sustains strength from faith. I will not be moved by these cynical would-be murderers. I will not turn my face from any warm ray of hope.

It felt in some ways unreal—siting there on the front lawn of the White House—among the world and national leaders. To our left, the Marine Band outfitted in brilliant red jackets, playing the traditional martial music of State occasions. To our right the Members of

Congress filed in, some laughing and chatting as though this were just another White House ceremony, others seeming always to have their heads pointed toward the television cameras. In front of us, the small table soon to be used for the signing, and just behind it the flags of the United States, Egypt and Israel flapping in a stiff breeze. And in back of us, across the street, stretched a sea of faces in beautiful Lafayette Park. Many in that park were not demonstrating against anything; maybe they were just curious; maybe, like us, they had come to see and hear some world leaders talk about hope and peace and brotherhood.

A beautiful female voice announced the three leaders. Suddenly everyone stood, and I missed the entrance. I couldn't see, and I was angry—not unlike the anger felt when someone blocks your view at the movies or at the theater. Emotions moved quickly. Barely had I time to feel guilty for what seemed like irreverent anger on such an occasion, when the band struck up the three national anthems. The first tears came with the opening strains of Hatikvah; there we all stood at attention, some of the Jews singing. Part way through, Israeli Prime Minister Begin's lips began to move to the words. (I opened to Begin's autobiography the next day to review the story of his having met a former Pravda editor aboard a Soviet slave ship. Begin tells that this man who had spent his life as a Communist, moving up the chain, was, when they met, "a broken man, a tormented prisoner, an enemy of the people, a degraded and broken Jew." As they sat together, these two men, the one who had since his childhood been a Jew in name only asked the other who all his life had been totally a Jew to sing for him the words of the Hatikvah. "Embedded in his memory," wrote Begin, "for more than thirty years were the first words of the line: 'To return to the land of our forefathers.'") There I stood, and beside me my wife, with the memories of Auschwitz seared inside her forever, and we watched and we listened as this Polish Jew—now the leader of the Jewish State—sang to the whole world the words of returning. Just one day earlier one of those oh-so-smart television reporters pressed Begin as to whether the treaty would be signed "for sure" the next day. Begin replied: "With God's help." The reporter asked whether Begin was being evasive. The Prime Minister answered: "Listen, my friend, ever since I was a young child, I was taught that nothing ever happens without God's help."

It occurred to me as we watched the three men sign the historic documents that if a person were to write a fictional account of such a happening, none of these leaders would be as they are. A short, bald man rooted in European Orthodox Jewish tradition? Unlikely. A smiling, pipe-puffing grandfather from Egypt, praising his friends Je-e-e-my and Menachem? Hardly. And an American president from the deep South who has often been characterized as not knowing his way around Washington much less the tangle of Mid-East problems? Never. Where are the Jew with the flowing mane of white hair, the Arab with his native dress and harem, the President loaded with charisma? History is not cast in the way movies or television drama are; there are events and, with God's help, the right people to deal with the events at the right time.

It will not be easy; one day does not erase years. As we, a group of Jews lucky enough to be invited, waited to be cleared through, this happened: A bus pulled up. Out moved a contingent of Arabic VIPs. They were quickly escorted inside. Someone in our crowd said: "Did you see what happened? They let the Egyptians get in first. What do they mean by that?" There is still a "they" and a "we" even among American Jews. Maybe, more so among American Jews.

It was interesting that the three leaders—Begin, Carter and Sadat— with all their own eloquence and their aides and writers, each chose to hearken back to Isaiah and the timeless promise and hope that "Nation shall not lift up sword against Nation, neither shall they learn war anymore." It is good that we can trace our roots back in common to such a thought, to such a philosophy, to such a prayer, even now when peace in the Middle East seems unreachable.

But, those years ago, as we walked slowly away from the White House after the ceremony was concluded, I thought to myself: "Can it be, despite all the obstacles, that the time has come to plant the seeds for peace in the world?" I pledged to myself on that spot to remember the words from Isaiah. To remember them in the face of the terrorist murderers. To remember them even as the prophets of doom tell us it is an illusion, this talk of peace. To remember them when there seems only a shadow of hope, and beyond. To remember those words even as I remember the six million Jews who were gone from this world, but who spoke through the lips of Begin when he said:

"No more bloodshed. Peace. Shalom. Salaam. Forever."

Fear and Shame:
Introduction to Hate

I t seems that as we grow older, the happy events of our lives meld into a pleasant, if hazy, melange, while the old fears and moments of terror take on sharp edges and surreal clarity. A face, a look, a visit to a house or a street remembered, and the tight feeling comes back in a rush. Even though the intervening years have removed the danger—the terror, shame, and confusion have not lost their bite.

I look back more than half a century to the dilemma of a Jewish boy facing anti-Semitism for the first time, a boy ashamed to confess his fear, and unable to overcome it. I still can feel the fear of a rather lonely twelve-year-old. I remember the evasions and deceptions, the feigned illnesses.

"Ma, my head feels hot. Please Ma, I don't wanna go to school today. I promise. My head is still hot, and I feel like throwing up."

But even when those strategies worked, they provided no long-term relief. As night came, as I lay in the dead silence of my tiny third-floor bedroom with the eaved walls, the fear returned with thoughts of tomorrow. I saw the face of The Boy, a few years older, a face with splotches and freckles along both cheeks. His brown hair was askew, and his teeth were rotting along the upper edges. He wore a moth-eaten brown sweater, and his green eyes threw off the unmistakable signs of hate.

I remember the look of hatred in those eyes on that long ago day as The Boy—I never learned his name—savagely punched my friend Rich, again and again, each time yelling: "The goddam Jews have all the money! The goddam Jews have all the money!" (I was too frightened at the time to appreciate the irony of the fact that my father was working twelve hours a day on a coal truck for about $20 a week.)

Rich had been caught in a lie. It was after school in the chill of an autumn day, and we were walking to Talmud Torah where, it was our parents' fervent hope, we would absorb some Jewish knowledge and culture, and prepare for Bar Mitzvah. The religious school was situated in a poor section of the city that included six kosher butchers, and several thousand Jews living mostly in three-decker tenements. The section was called Suffolk Square, but it was known by many non-Jews, and without affection, as Jew Town.

As Rich and I rounded a corner, The Boy and three of his cohorts approached us.

"Where are you guys going?"

With no sense of heroism, but because I was carrying Hebrew books under my arm, I answered, "I'm going to Hebrew school."

The question was repeated to Rich. "I don't go to Hebrew school. I'm just walking him down," he said, pointing to me.

"You a Jew?"

"No. I'm Protestant," was Rich's shaky reply.

"What church you go to?"

"St. Mary's."

The last syllable was barely out of his mouth before Rich was on the ground, writhing in pain. The Boy's fist had shot out quickly, and caught him in the stomach. Even I knew that St. Mary's was a Catholic church.

One of The Boy's friends came over to me. "What's a-matter, Jewboy, why don't you help your friend?" I was frozen in fear and couldn't answer.

That's when the feeling of terror started; I think it was just at that moment. "Come on, why don't you belt me? You're bigger than I am. You yellow? Come on, unless you say you're yellow, I'm going to give you just what your friend is getting." By this time The Boy was sitting astride Rich, beating on his head, first with one hand, then with the other. At his command, my friend was groaning, "I'm a Jew. I'm a Jew."

My oppressor moved closer, and began circling me, his fists fixed in the classic boxer's position. After what seemed like hours, I heard myself say, softly, "I'm yellow." By this time, The Boy had tired of his sport with Rich, climbed off his stomach, and walked toward me. "What about him?" he asked. "He just told me he's yellow; besides he admitted that he's a Jew," said my tormentor, seeming almost to take my side.

"Okay," the Boy said, "you guys get your asses outa here , and don't ever walk by this corner again. Understand?" As we ran toward Almont

Street and the cheder they yelled after us: "Heil Hitler, Jews. Heil Hitler."

Rich, his clothing torn and face bruised, told all to his parents, and from that day his mother accompanied him to and from Hebrew school. I told no one, and for reasons not too clear, I refused to walk protected by Rich's mother. So I found a new route to Hebrew school, and traveled it alone. It took about 15 minutes longer, but except for one incident when he hurled rocks at my head, I avoided any further encounters with The Boy.

But my feeling of relief was shattered one day not long after when I saw The Boy playing basketball in my schoolyard. He was going to the same school, and I had never noticed him! He didn't see me. I hid out in my back yard later that day, instead of going to Hebrew school, not trusting my new route.

I saw The Boy only once more, several years later, on a bus. I'm certain he had no idea who I was. By that time, the fear had submerged, but not the shame. For three years after I had spotted him in the schoolyard, I was afraid. Until I had graduated from the Hebrew and junior high schools, I was afraid. And through those years, as I became taller and stronger, as my voice deepened, as I became a Bar Mitzvah, I was ashamed. And still I shared my feelings with no one. It was as a young man of 16 that I broke through the shame that had sat like a lump inside my stomach.

My parents, after saving for years, finally were able to afford their first home. It was a somewhat run-down, two-family house they purchased in a neighborhood where few Jews lived.

After spending the first night in our new home, I walked out the front door in the morning on my way to school. There, scrawled all over the sidewalk and street, in huge, chalked letters, were the words: "Get out, kikes, Jews not wanted here."

The fear came flooding back, and the shame. But this time it was different. There were stirrings of anger. This time it wasn't secret, something done just to me. This time it was connected to my parents, with our family, and in that post-war year of 1947, with all the Jews. I did my best to rub out the hateful words with hands full of dirt and the soles of my shoes. While there were no further incidents, my anger mounted, but there seemed no one to strike back at.

Then on Halloween night, as I walked toward my new house with a friend, returning from a party, I heard noises from across the street, cat-calls and whistles. Suddenly, a flashlight beam hit me full in the face. "Come on over here, Jew-boy." A familiar feeling came over me, as my companion ran off up the street, leaving me alone on the sidewalk. "Look at that dirty Jew-boy. Come over here, kike."

There were five of them sitting on a low wall. I could see only their outlines in the moonless night, but I could imagine their faces. "Come on over and get some, Jew."

Suddenly, and without thought, I sucked in the night air, and yelled back: "You bastards come over here one at a time and say that."

I stood rooted for what seemed an eternity. The boys giggled and whispered among themselves, but said nothing more to me. Silently they got up from the wall and walked single file around the corner, and out of my sight.

I stood there alone, savoring a new feeling, one that would stay with me the rest of my life. Then I turned and walked slowly toward my house, whistling softly between my teeth, the way I always did when I felt good.

The Bitter and the Sweet

The long-term memory plays tricks. A wondrous clarity here. A shadowy recollection there. A magical vaulting backward a half century to a time and place now existing only in the mind's eye. As the Jewish holidays—especially Rosh Hashanah and Yom Kippur—approach each year, an over-sensitive young boy is confused and unhappy. He lives, in the late 1930s, amid a spread of Jewish lifestyles too broad for his understanding.

In his six-room flat lives his great grandfather, his grandparents, his parents, and his brother. From these socially-conscious, caring and unprejudiced people would spring his later connections with the poor, the underdogs and the underprivileged. The Yiddishe tam—the Jewish inside feeling—and the memories, he would collect from his other grandparents, the religious ones, the Zaydie and the Bubbie.

It is at their ramshackle, two-family home, pressed between the railroad tracks and a working-class bar, and, of course, within walking distance of Bas Yisroal Synagogue, where the memories are permanently etched.

The holidays in particular are locked into tastes and smells and textures. A crunchy red apple wedge dipped into a clear glass bowl of honey. A chunk of yellow challah, yanked from a huge round loaf studded with raisins. The Passover wine, blood red, aged in a white porcelain vat on the glassed-in back porch. Hamentaschen so rich and soft, thousands of coagulated poppy seeds surrounded by a sweet brown crust. Piles of potato pancakes fried by Bubbie at the old kerosene stove, downed with "oohs and aahs" by the boy, his father and his Uncle Sammy. The sukkah, built against the back wall of that bar.

Memories as sweet as the new-year honey. But with the good and the awesome came also the awful. On the High Holy Days, a terrible embarrassment for the boy, forced to sit in the synagogue—for all to see—on a small wooden box wedged between his father's wall seat and a steam radiator. But even the embarrassment provided relief from the palpable boredom of listening, hour after hour, to the cryptic prayers mumbled by swaying, old men wrapped in their fringed shawls.

Little respite was available for the boy, even when he was permitted to take a break in the tiny yard. There he had to fight the Christian kids, who were incensed that this participant in deicide also was able to miss school for two days. The boy tested his God on Yom Kippur—the holy fast day—by smoking Old Gold cigarettes behind the ice house up the street from the synagogue.

He was vaguely disappointed that this major sin brought no discernible retribution. Instead, this early Jewish life of contradiction, embarrassment and anger, formed all that was good in the man who emerged—his idealism, his social action, his spirituality, his head full of questions and ideas. For those diverse and confusing people were, after all, doing their best, and each of them in a way that was decidedly Jewish.

So, in his present life, as he prepares for the High Holy Days, how is it different? As the man who was that boy, let me tell you. While my Jewish practices and lifestyle may be more consistent and positive, I am not certain they are as meaningful. There is a certain emptiness, born of an intellect and skepticism that replaced acceptance and a bit of fear. There is too much head and not enough *hertz* and *neshama*, heart and soul.

Thus, as the Days of Awe near, I am filled with reluctance and ambivalence. My boyhood memories seem sweeter with passing time, while my current experiences fail to live up to my—perhaps unrealistic—expectations. Of course, neither do I live up to the expectations my religion has for me.

It is a typical Jewish puzzle, so I posit this Jewish-type solution: I will not expect too much from God, if God does not expect too much from me.

A Jew Considers Christmas

. . . No-el, No-el, born is the King of Is-rye-al.

I t is mid-October. I am tuned in to a re-run of Mary Tyler Moore on Nickelodeon. During a commercial break I hear for the first time, the sounds of a Christmas carol. They're selling one of those re-cycled Yuletide records, crooned by a passé Western singer.

I am angry and, almost immediately afterward, guilty. I know that Christmas is an important and meaningful time of the year for all the Christians I know and care about. I also know that this is the time of the year when, despite all my inter-faith activities and my lifelong Christian friendships, I will feel alienated, lonely and outside the mainstream of my country and my community.

It does not help that Christians, because they care, will attempt to equate Christmas with Hanukah, a relatively minor Jewish observance. For me, this good-faith effort only emphasizes the unbridged gap. Christmas is unique in imposing this sense of otherness on me. Easter, for example, should be more alien to me as a Jew, symbolizing as it does the resurrection of Jesus. But it isn't. In my activities in the local interfaith council, I frequently attend Christian churches. I am often moved by the words of the clergy, and I feel welcome and at home in these congregations. My membership in a Jewish-Christian partnership group is unifying, and our dialogues are frank and enlightening.

Thus I have concluded it is the secularization of Christmas, not just its religious significance to Christians, that causes my pain. I am unable to escape Christmas with its twin messages: A religious message that my beliefs and those of other non-Christians are not valid, are outmoded, have been replaced by a new truth. And a secular message that celebrating Christmas is part of the American experience, that there is a two-month period of shameless commercialism every year in which one either participates or feels like an outsider.

This situation is much worse for young non-Christians. I remember as a kid in a working-class city, Christmas season frightened and confused me. Most of my closest friends were Christians. While our differences were always apparent, it was not until Christmastime that they became overwhelming and divisive.

There was I, studying six days a week in an after-school Hebrew School, trying to learn a strange, squiggly-lined language and hearing the sad stories of the Hebrew Testament. There was my pal, Charlie Perry, free from religious encumbrances after school and attending church sporadically, being rewarded with Christmas, with all its presents and pageantry and its seemingly easy to understand message.

Public school was no better. Write an essay on what you are going to do on your Christmas vacation. What do you want from Santa Claus? The Christmas decorations. The assemblies to hear the school choir sing its Christmas concert. Occasionally they would throw in a Hanukah song, which only served to embarrass me. In my college years, you really were not part of the in group if you didn't attend Midnight Mass at the cathedral.

In the office, Christmas party and gift exchange planning got underway in late Fall. There was much talk about "getting into the spirit of the season," which always seemed in a certain way to be saying it's okay to forget the Christian message of love for the rest of the year but to work on one's behavior in November and December.

Television also pays its annual homage to the season. Just about every show starts shifting into Christmas mode by early December. There are the Christmas specials. Commercials are tilted to the season. And, of course, the Christmas records for sale.

Downtown, there is the huge tree in the square. The reindeer and sleds sit atop every street light. Then there is always the Battle of the Crèche. To me, this goes beyond the Constitutional tenet about separation of church and state. I cannot believe there is true religious feeling about having holy imagery stuck on the front lawn of city hall or the state house (and that includes the practice of the Lubovich sect of erecting giant Hanukah menorahs on public places across the nation).

There is a certain beauty, purity and heightening of the human spirit in the religious observance of Christmas. It advances a feeling of equality among all people, of seeking peace above war, of practicing true charity and compassion.

The "public" Christmas presents us with religion stripped of its spiritual meaning and true message, sanitized and force-fed to a nation based on both guaranteeing a free expression of faith and keeping it separate from the state. If there is a hope that we will solve our major problems, overcome our hates and prejudices, it surely lies in recognizing those values we hold in common and using those things to bring our nation and world together.

The injection of Christmas, made crass and commercial, into the secular life of our society does nothing to advance this goal.

50 Years Later—
the Scourge of Jew-hatred
Continues

I cannot remain silent. I cannot live while the rest of the Jewish people in Poland, whom I represent, continue to be liquidated.

My companions of the Warsaw Ghetto fell in a last heroic battle with their weapons in their hands. I did not have the honor to die with them but I belong to them to their common grave.

Let my death be an energetic cry of protest against the indifference of the world which witnesses the extermination of the Jewish people without taking any steps to prevent it. In our day and age human life is of little value; having failed to achieve success in my life, I hope that my death may jolt the indifference of those who perhaps even in this extreme moment, could save the Jews who are still alive in Poland.

Samuel Zygelbojm, 1943

(Excerpt from a letter he wrote before committing suicide)

As a representative of the Polish Jews, Samuel Arthur Zygelbojm joined the National Polish Committee which eventually became the Polish Government in Exile. During his stay in London, he did everything in his power to draw the attention of the world to the fate of the Jews under Nazi occupation, but was unable to obtain any reaction.

Zygelbojm's words, all these years later, tell us of tragedy piled upon tragedy; of a world unconcerned with the mass murder of Jews; of world leaders who found excuse after excuse to delay while they abetted in the deaths of six million innocent human beings.

Despite Zygelbojm laying down his life, the deaths continued unabated. Yet, in some awful ways, death was not the worst. It was the manner of death, the days leading up to it. It was the fruitlessness of such death, the innocence of the victims. It was the loss of dignity, of humanity. It was the children seeing their parents naked and cowering in fear and shame. It was parents knowing their beloved children would be starved and beaten and, finally, murdered—and knowing they had no power to do anything about it. Think about it, mothers and fathers, think about it.

It was Orthodox Jews knowing the horror that after their deaths there would be no ritual cleansing of their bodies, no proper burial, no Kaddish intoned over them. It was trying to figure out what they had done to displease God enough that He should abandon them.

It was diarrhea with no toilets or paper. It was living in filth, with no soap or water. It was degradation. It was subjugation. It was torture. It was mutilation. It was loss of control over one's life. It was wondering where the world was, why no one came to help.

One prisoner from Dachau, a survivor, related this story: "The SS guards took pleasure in telling us that we had no chance of coming out alive, a point they emphasized with particular relish by insisting that, after the war, the rest of the world would not believe what happened; there would be rumors, speculation, but no clear evidence, and people would conclude that evil on such a scale was not possible."

Lest you think that such predictions could not come true, that people could doubt the Holocaust, let me tell you that just some four decades after that woman's story, a prominent American wrote these words: "Half the survivors' testimonies at Yad Vashem are unreliable." And he wrote further: ". . . people who claim to be survivors of Hitler's death camps suffer from Holocaust survivor syndrome and are afflicted with group fantasies of martyrdom and heroics."

The writer of those words said: "I don't have anything to apologize for." He is Patrick J. Buchanan, the man who won the 1996 New Hampshire presidential primary, to the endless shame of that backward state and every person who voted for him. Shame on those of us who supported him, for whatever reason, and shame on those of us who didn't fight him hard enough. It is after all, through the inaction of good people that evil finds a rooting place.

And it is Marlon Brando who says, "Hollywood is run by Jews. It's owned by Jews, and they should have a greater sensitivity about the issue of people who are suffering." *People who are suffering?* This is a sot who became famous and very wealthy thanks to Jewish-owned Hollywood, and then debauched himself and his talent. If he refers to

Caucasian suffering, no group has suffered more over the past two thousand years than the Jews themselves. If he means African Americans, no group has made a greater commitment of personal involvement, resources and even lives than did the Jews during the Civil Rights revolution and after. Of course, Brando said his comments were not meant to be anti-Semitic.

It is Polish ultra-nationalists marching outside the gates of Auschwitz, all upset over a ban on constructing a mini-mall near the death camp remains. Do you suppose these people whose parents never were able to figure out what caused all that smoke and ashes 50 years ago— do you suppose these people want to come to the Auschwitz neighborhood to buy their cigarettes and beer? Or could there be another reason. Do they want to dishonor even the shards of bones and the dust of one and one half million Jews murdered there, and still swirling around in that huge, ungodly cemetery?

It is the Stars of David spray-painted with angry words on the wall of Jewish owned business. It is the still unsolved crimes of the haters who drew swastikas and wrote "Jews drink blood," on the roof of my synagogue.

It was the person who admonished me several years ago, after Jesse Jackson call New York City "Hymie town," that "you people sometimes are just too sensitive."

Deborah Lipstadt, a talented Holocaust chronicler, felt forced against her own better instincts, to write a book called "Denying the Holocaust, The Growing Assault on Truth and Memory." Here is a brief passage from the book:

"Deniers acknowledge that some Jews were incarcerated in places such as Auschwitz, but they maintain, as they did at the trail of a Holocaust denier in Canada, it was equipped with 'all the luxuries of a country club' including a swimming pool, dance hall, and recreational facilities. Some Jews may have died, they said, but this was the natural consequence of wartime deprivations.

"The central assertion of the deniers is that Jews are not victims, but victimizers. They 'stole' billions in reparations, destroyed Germany's good name by spreading the 'myth' of the Holocaust, and won international sympathy because of what they claimed had been done to them."

Canadian newspapers covering the 1985 trail carried headlines such as "Nazi Camp had Pool, Ballroom," and "Prisoners at Auschwitz dined, danced to band, Zundel Witness Testifies."

So, if the Holocaust never occurred, what happened to the six million people? And where are the children? The 1.5 million Jewish children slaughtered in the Holocaust would today be in their 50s and 60s, enjoying their own children, and even grandchildren. Instead we have only the memories of them, and some drawings and writing left behind.

It is difficult to live in a world where, fifty years later, there are those—in growing numbers—who would deny Jews even their own sorrow, the right to mourn in peace. The right of six million souls to rest. They have no graves, no places in tree-lined cemeteries like their oppressors. They are fading memories.

We must not allow this to happen. We must honor them both in memory and by the way we lead our lives and teach our children to lead theirs. This is true for all of us, whatever our faith. But it is particularly true of Jews because we carry a special burden, and a special responsibility to make of these martyred millions a living *b'racha*, a blessing.

The sage Hillel said long ago: "In a place where no one behaves like a human being, you must strive to be human!" Can we not agree at least and at last to strive to be human?

Farrakhan is Vile, Pure and Simple

Louis Farrakhan is a bigot, a racist, an anti-Semite, a hate-peddler. And, no matter how hard the supporters of his vaunted Million Man March in Washington try to justify it, his means do not justify their ends. Their support of the movement Farrakhan leads is shameful and unacceptable.

I was there that hot August day in 1963 when Martin Luther King Jr. stood before a hopeful throng of all ages, colors and religions. And I do not remember Dr. King referring to Judaism as a "gutter religion" as Farrakhan has. And I do not remember Dr. King referring to Jews as "bloodsuckers" as Louis Farrakhan has.

I do remember Martin King praying, instead, for that day when all people would come together in peace and love, when all children, his and mine, could play together with no fear or hatred between them.

Asked to comment on his "bloodsucker" reference, Farrakhan said his words were used "out of context to create division," and the march is "for the suffering of all black men." Change the word black to Aryan, and we hear terrible and frightening echoes of Nazi Minister of Information Joseph Goebbels. The despicable Farrakhan went farther, saying "poor Jews died while big Jews were at the root of what you call the Holocaust."

Americans have a notoriously short memory bank and, too often abetted by the media, reconstruct our home-grown bigots or allow them to be redefined. Patrick Buchanan, who won a Republican presidential primary in New Hampshire, is a sorry and frightening example.

Buchanan is usually described in the media as "a commentator," and certainly that is true. But he also is an unapologetic xenophobe, homophobe and anti-Semite. If the media chooses, by its omissions, to help legitimize Buchanan, it is up to the rest of us to remember what he has said, written and never recanted.

The same is true in the case of Farrakhan. Merely because he and his vast public relations machinery have opted to recast his image makes Farrakhan no less a charlatan.

The late Barbara Tuchman, a brilliant biographer and historian, said that anti-Semitism has nothing to do with the acts or behavior of Jews; rather it is based upon the needs of the oppressor. So it was during the Inquisition. So it was in Nazi Germany. So it is with Farrakhan. Scapegoats were needed; scapegoats were found. They were the Jews.

I accuse those who are complicit with the hate-spewer Farrakhan by either their timidity or through statements that they agree with his ends if not his means. I accuse Jesse Jackson. I accuse Rep. Donald Payne, head of the Congressional Black Caucus. I accuse Philadelphia Mayor Edward Rendell, a white Jew. I accuse District of Columbia Mayor Marion Barry. I accuse ousted NAACP head Benjamin Chavis. And I applaud the national NAACP for withholding its support.

One wonders what the uproar, particularly from the left, might have been had a national figure called the woman's movement a "gutter" movement. Or people who run abortion clinics "bloodsuckers." Or blamed Native Americans for their massacre at the hands of white Americans.

Speaking as a Jew, past 70, I am finally done with both being an apologist and having to listen to apologists. These are the kinds of things I have had to hear all my life:

"Well when I said he Jewed me down, I really didn't mean a Jew like you . . ." "You know, Jewish American princess only is about those pushy types from Los Angeles and New York City."

"When Jesse Jackson called New York, 'Hymie Town,' that was in a private conversation; and besides you Jews sometimes are just too sensitive."

"People who claim to be survivors of Hitler's death camps suffer from Holocaust survivor syndrome and are afflicted with group fantasies of martyrdom and heroics." (A quote from Patrick Buchanan)

Jews have stood at the center of just about every civil and human rights movement in this nation and others. And while we certainly have been imperfect and made errors, we have put our time, our money, and our lives forward. Of the three young civil rights workers who were murdered in Philadelphia, Mississippi, let us not forget that two of them were Jews.

The day after the assassination of Martin Luther King, three officials from the Small Business Administration took their lives in their hands by attending a meeting of several hundred angry blacks to assist those whose businesses had gone up in smoke in the District of Columbia ghetto. All three of us were Jews.

It was my privilege to be part of the U.S. Senate team, under the leadership of Sen. Hubert Humphrey, who fought for passage of the historic 1964 Civil Right legislation. It was my honor each year to participate in Martin Luther King day inter-faith activities, and to demand that New Hampshire put its shame behind it and enact a King holiday.

I cite these things not to establish my "liberal credentials," but to point out that my religion has taught me that justice must "well up like mighty waters . . . ."

Many people of good will were deeply saddened by the break-up of the Black-Jewish coalition which had done so much good work in furthering the civil rights movement. And, despite the fracture, many Jews—myself included—have continued in the fight against the virtual slavery that still exists in the black ghettos across America.

But, at the same time, I will also fight against the demagogues who despoil the memories of the 6 million murdered Jews—1.5 million of them children—by saying it all was our fault. I will fight the bigots and the haters and the dividers. I refuse to stand aside, either in the name of black brotherhood or the call for a Christian America, while Jews and Judaism are reviled and scapegoated to meet the hateful and perverted ends of the Farrakhans and Buchanans.

It is time to cast them, and all like them, out into the ash-heap of history where they belong.

Making Common Cause:
A Global Jewish View

My friend Joe is blind. My friend Marcus is gay. My friend Kathi is a woman. My friend Bill is a conservative Republican. My tenants are fundamentalist Christians. My friend Phil is Catholic. My doctor is Protestant. Frank is homeless. My brother lived in a state school for the mentally retarded. My friend Steve is a 29-year-old teacher. Mel and I have known each other for 30 plus years. He is black. Skye is a Pagan. My dear old friend Harry is an atheist. My buddy Walter is a Lutheran pastor. Bob is a gay minister. Karen is a divorcee. Eva is a Socialist. And Julie is dying of cancer.

What have all these statements to do with making common cause? Just everything. For I believe, as much as I believe anything, that if each of us got to know one of every person different from us, hatred and bigotry and scape-goating would disappear. Seem like a miracle? Hardly. Rather I see it as the single most pragmatic approach to the enormous challenge of learning to live together—peacefully and comfortably.

More than 50 years ago in an industrial city outside Boston, I am walking fast, making my way to Hebrew School one afternoon, hugging the inside of the sidewalk to make myself less visible. But it doesn't work.

I hear the familiar yell, "Hey, Jew boy, wait up." I know it is the boy with the ugly green teeth and his little band of toughs. I know they will beat me physically and verbally. And they do.

It is not until a long time after that I was able to consider what happened rationally, and decide what to do about it. For years I have wished that somehow I could bump into the boy with the green teeth—like me, an aging man by now, and tell him this: "If only we had known each other better, or if our parents were friends, it would have been different. If only we had known each other, I could have explained who Hitler was and what he was doing to kids like us who were Jewish and, in some cases, Catholic, like you. If only we had played tag together, and shared dreams, like I did with my closest friend, Charlie Perry, a Christian like you, we could have formed an alliance against the evil and greedy people who were keeping us down. If only . . ."

I never did get to talk to that kid again, but I pledged to work to break through the hatred and intolerance I believe is not born into anyone, but is bred—to some degree—into each of us. But before we can reach that exalted goal, we must have the courage to look at ourselves and our own biases and wash them away. It is fairly easy to do this intellectually, since clearly prejudice is a social and religious and moral and ethical flaw. But that is not enough; we must move from the thinking of the mind to the feeling of the heart. There is a Hebrew word: rachmonis, which means to have compassion, moving a step beyond sympathy to empathy . . . to an understanding of the pain that hatred causes . . . to a sharing of that pain . . . to the joy of discovery that we really all are both different and alike . . . to the understanding that we can live with our differences if we learn to live and work together and even to love each other for those universal things we hold in common.

The real differences in this world are not the language we speak or what faith we practice or what color we are; rather they are the social and economic injustices that divide people from people, race from race, economic classes from each other. These are the areas in which we must work. If we have to hate something, let it be poverty and child hunger and homelessness and war and the use of ethnicity or religion or wealth as reasons for superiority over others. We should not use as a way to feel morally superior, for example, a 14-year-old ghetto girl with a child of her own, who is uneducated, downtrodden and frightened to death. Such feelings are inhuman and will only serve to separate us more, turning our hearts to stone.

We must learn the best that our religions preach, and practice those things, because, after all, it is the act that counts. How do we make common cause? First, by a recognition of our shared humanity, complete with its foibles, weaknesses and its ability to transcend, and seek higher purpose. For if we profess a belief in something bigger and better than we, something to reach for, then surely it is a blasphemy of the highest order not to live together in respect and even affection. I believe that is the closest we can come to God.

If Not Now, When?

T
hank you for the honor and the responsibility of sharing some thoughts—and worshipping with you—this day. My connection with this Unitarian church has been long and happy.

The title of this sermon came from the famous quote of the wise rabbi of old, Hillel: "If I am not for myself, who will be for me? But if I am only for myself, what am I? And if not now, when?" These are sage, but frightening words, for they place the responsibility squarely with each of us . . . the responsibility to search for the right thing to do, and then do it.

You may wonder why I have chosen to discuss subjects so negative and unpleasant—the effect of greed upon our nation and its people, and the pandering to it by all too many of those we elect to represent us in government. Why? Because, clearly, this is a moral question and there is no better place than a church to face a moral question, and no better group of people than mainline congregations to call upon for an intelligent and unrelenting opposition to what is happening to America today.

Voices scream out for help, but their words are lost in a welter of acquisition, accumulation and an artless and greedy climb to make the Forbes Magazine most wealthy list. The free market is by itself end-lessly greedy and acquisitive, after all. Left to its own devices, it will take and take. Thus I believe one of the important tasks of government is to regulate and restrain—but not choke—the avidity of the market, and keep it somewhere with the bounds of reason and decency.

In recent years, those reins on the market have, to a great extent, been loosened. While a lot of small investors may have benefited from this situation, the main result has been to enrich enormously the already rich. This situation, along with the cruel and callous freebooters who are in charge of Washington, have cast this nation into two Americas. One America is of the rich-rich who,increasingly, live in walled communities, protected by private goon squads, and wearing fancy clothes paid for with the sweat of children in Mexico, China and

India, who are held in virtual slavery producing the goods that buy the good life for the few on the top of the pyramid.

The other America is comprised of the disappearing middle class, whose jobs are at the mercy of stockholders' greed, whose kids won't make it to college, and whose futures have been mortgaged on the altar of a balanced budget, huge congressional pensions, and hundreds of billions in giveaways to corporate America. And, oh, yes, the other America includes, as it always has, the increasingly more despised poor.

The influence of the rich upon the engines of American politics and government is more pronounced today than it has been perhaps ever. Too many of our elected representatives have become mere toadies to the rich, developing a slave-like dependency upon their dollars.

This Sodom and Gomorrah on the Potomac has given birth to one of the cruel ironies of our time: The more wealth becomes concentrated among fewer and fewer, the more the blame for the negative effects of this orgy of greed are placed on the poor.

And who has financed this gold strike for the wealthy? Why, the working middle-class, of course. Words like downsizing and outplacement made their way into the vocabulary. The layoffs and firings are in the millions. Loyal employees cruelly fired, not because of poor quality work, not even necessarily because their companies were losing money. No, these working people—the kind who used to make a career in one company—were sacrificed, thrown into the flaming volcano to feed the insatiable market, whose altar-boy, Dow Jones, erupted upward.

So, while the rich get richer, and over $150 billion pours into defense contractors and giant corporations in tax breaks and subsidies, our leading preachers of virtue and value have chosen the black ghetto mother and her innocent kids as the enemies of America's future. Bill Clinton joined hands with Newt Gingrich and their ilk, to "end welfare as we know it." I agree, only I demand from these snake-oil salesmen that we end welfare starting at the top. I am damn sick and tired of subsidizing the bomb makers, the tobacco industry, chemical companies and all the rest. It's time Dwayne Andreas of Archer Daniel Midland and his protégé, Bob Dole, stood on their own two feet. Same with Clinton and the chicken industry.

Currently, there is no united force to expose these insanities and abuses of our tax dollars. I fear we can expect little help from those currently in power, since they pretty much all feed from the trough. So, it is we who must create an opposing force. We must muster the courage and determination to demand justice and fairness, and to expose the dark alliances that block our access to our own government. We must face the perpetrators and say: No more!

But, in the final analysis it will not be enough to expose the worst in the worst of us. It is more important to bring out the best in the best of us, and then move to action.

First, we must learn the facts, educate ourselves so that we can no longer be pushed aside with glib and false arguments. We must, as did Dr. King and Bobby Kennedy, go among the poor, the homeless, the helpless and the oppressed. We must learn to understand the fear and anger in a young life that is constantly in danger, that is lived minute-by-minute with an empty belly, an infected body and a mind dulled by hopelessness and despair.

Then we must learn and know and believe that the 14-year-old black girl in the ghetto, who has made a baby to prove she exists and to have something to love, is not the enemy, not our enemy. And we must learn and know and believe that there is an ungodly connection between the pain and suffering of 14 million poor kids and the orgy of greed and cold-heartedness that is turning this society to stone.

Then we will be ready for an oath, this oath: Not one more child— black, brown, yellow, red or white—shall we allow to starve or freeze, or be gnawed by rats, or be forced by a life of desperation into early death by drugs or a bullet. None of these obscenities shall again occur in the name of a Dow Jones uptick, or a tax cut, or a balanced budget, or an Armani suit or a Mercedes.

For even one starving child is too many. One body frozen beside a railroad track or under a bridge is too many. One mother whose milk is laced with crack is too many. One AIDS baby is too many. And one among us—the fortunate—who does nothing but weep and feel guilty is too many.

So what do we say about these things to those who rule? Those who assure us the poor love their poverty. That the poor—especially the poor black—are by nature morally and intellectually inferior to the rest of us. What shall we say to those who are destroying the human face of government in the name of balancing numbers on a piece of paper, an act that in itself will change nothing?

I would demand of them all, the cynics, the hypocrites, the wafflers and the fast talkers—I would demand that these self-righteous, well-to-do white men immediately make available documents that will verify how much of their fortunes they have given to charity over the past ten years. And, further, how many hours of their time they have volunteered at a soup kitchen, a homeless shelter or in a ghetto.

We must tell them—and ourselves—that it is not enough to talk the talk; we must also walk the walk. In Judaism, we are taught that the act is everything, that helping one in need is the highest calling, doing God's work. It takes precedence over all other duties.

Let me tell you a story to illustrate this point. In a small Polish city many years ago, there lived a Rabbi who was renowned for his piety and strict adherence to the 613 commandments from God to live as a religious Jew. Needless to say, the members of his congregation cherished the Rabbi, and often bragged about him to folks in neighboring communities.

Then one year, something unimaginable happened. The Rabbi was late for the beginning of services on Yom Kippur morning. Now, Yom Kippur is the holiest of days, sometimes referred to as the Sabbath of Sabbaths. So when the Rabbi was late, it was feared that he was ill. But he showed up in good health, and even more holy than ever.

After the same occurrence on the second year, the leaders of the synagogue vowed to seek the answer. Of course, they could not ask the Rabbi—one did not speak directly to a holy man, not until spoken to. And so the next Yom Kippur morning, the president of the congregation hid in the bushes outside the Rabbi's home, and waited.

Suddenly the Rabbi emerged dressed in his everyday clothes, his work clothes, and carrying a length of rope. The man could not believe his eyes. After all, working on the Sabbath of Sabbath's would break one of the major commandments. The Rabbi walked into the woods, and the man followed. The Rabbi began to pick up small branches, tied them into a bundle, and carried them on his back still deeper into the forest. Soon, he came to a run-down shack, with holes in the roof and a piece of burlap for a door. The Rabbi entered; the man sneaked up to the shack and peered inside.

There, lying on the bed was a frail, old woman covered only by a worn and dirty blanket. The Rabbi greeted her in Polish, which meant she was not Jewish. Then, to the horror of the man watching, the Rabbi took a loaf of bread from his jacket—my God, he thought, carrying food on this holiest of fast days!—and handed it to the old woman. Then he undid the bundle, stuffed the branches into a small stove, and lit a fire, breaking still another commandment.

The Rabbi squeezed the old woman's hand, left the shack and headed back to his home to put on his holiday clothes.

The president of the synagogue was confused and afraid. But suddenly, a light dawned and a smile spread across his face, and as he headed back to his prayer, he said in a voice now filled with joy: "Surely we have the most pious Rabbi in all of Poland."

We, too, can make such pious choices. The next time you are in a setting with one of our leaders, and they spout meaningless, mindless and unworkable solutions, challenge them, demand a direct answer. Yes, if necessary, raise your voice to be heard. Good manners are not a higher calling than feeding hungry children.

It won't be easy to do at first, but it will be right. It might help to picture in your mind's eye the first time Gandhi sat down, alone, on the ground, and refused to be moved. Or Nelson Mandela's first hour of his 27 years in prison. Or the first time Dr. King stood eye-to-eye with Sheriff Bull Connor. Or the black students pushing their way through an angry crowd at Little Rock High School. They all were frightened and unsure, but they were tired of it, just as tired as Rosa Park's feet were that day in the front of the bus. And when you get the garbage about downsizing the federal government, about how state governments and the private sector will be closer to the people, here are some questions to ask:

- Would state governments have ended slavery?
- Would the free market have established minimum wage or child labor laws? Or health, safety and environmental protections?
- Would the Alabama State Police or the Little Rock local cops have done a better job of protecting civil rights than the National Guard?
- Would state legislatures have passed uniform voting rights and public accommodation statutes?

- Would Wall Street have established Head Start or the Peace Corps, or Pell higher education assistance programs?
- Would the millions of people living in the boondocks have electricity yet without REA? Would local businesses fund Meals on Wheels or school lunch programs?
- Would the Bill of Rights exist if it had been left up to the city council or lobbyists or business and industry spokesmen?
- What would the interest rate on your house be if it were left to banks to control the money supply and set rates? Would local banks or local government insure your savings and deposits?
- How long would it take you to drive to Boston and New York on back roads if the federal highway system did not exist? How much state road improvement would there be without federal funding?
- How clean would our water be if industrial polluters were not regulated? How protected our forests and birds and animals if it were left to local hunting and lumber interests, and their state lobbies?
- Want to forego your Social Security checks and your Medicare protection against bankruptcy by illness?
- Would the states have gotten us to the moon, or financed cures for polio?
- And try to picture this: When all the programs have been passed along from federal to state to local, and the money doesn't match the programs—How much do you think your local taxes will be then?

Once we have learned our lessons and overcome our fright, then each of us must become a spokesperson for one poor child. Let us learn and repeat to those in power the words choking inside every ghetto mother who has seen her child gunned down. Let us—parents so proud of our children—speak out for a parent who has seen the bright light of intelligence and promise in her kid turn to bitterness and despair at the lack of opportunity. Let our voices become their voices.

Let us challenge the fortunate and powerful to meet their responsibilities. As John Kennedy once said: "Our privileges can be no greater than our obligations."

So, Archer Daniels Midland, you make billions in the food business and get millions in government subsidies. Do more to feed the hungry.

Physicians and insurance companies who have become wealthy with new opportunities, invest a few hundred thousand dollars in the communities that have made you rich and set up free clinics for the uninsured.

Gap, help clothe the unclothed.

Attorneys, make up the cut in Legal Services.

Homebuilders who made millions in low-income housing, help house the homeless now.

NBC, CBS, ABC, stop teaching kids about greed and violence and mindless sex; especially poor kids.

Elected officials, tell us what you have done in your pre-political lives for the poor and the needy. Explain how you will stop the continuing re-distribution of wealth away from the disappearing middle class upward to the rich.

Now my friends, if Jesus were sitting among us today, what might he tell us? Perhaps words like these: "Whatsoever you do for the least of these, you have done for me." And Isaiah, if he were here, might repeat his admonition to the greedy and power hungry: "It is you who have ravaged the vineyard; that which was robbed from the poor is in your houses. How dare you crush my people and grind the faces of the poor, says my God, the Eternal."

Or what might we hear from Martin King, or Gandhi or Lincoln? They turned compassion and empathy into action. Too many of our heroes paid with their lives, and we felt left adrift without them. Overcome in our grief at their deaths, we forgot the message of their lives:

One person can make a difference.

One person can make a difference.

One person can make a difference.

Indeed, if we are to reach such worthy goals, each person must make a difference.

Ignazio Silone, in "Bread and Wine," his novel of revolution and faith in the midst of Italian fascism, put it this way: "In every dictatorship, just one man, even any little man at all, who continues to think with his own head, puts the whole public order in danger . . . it's enough that a little man, just one little man, says NO for that formidable granite order to be in danger."

We live in times that cry out for thundering giants, but that seem to produce only mewling midgets. So, finally, it is up to us. We must act. We must become giants. We must reach deep inside ourselves and find the courage and the goodness of heart so that we—each and every one—becomes Silone's "any little man." And when we have the strength, let us try not only to convince evil people to do good. We must also make the moral decision to, ourselves, help bring positive change.

Some starts have been made. For example, Bishop Anthony Pilla, of Cleveland, as head of the Catholic Bishops association, said the church must become the political voice for the poor. These are his words: "Someone has to imagine a world where there is no more poverty, where there is no more homelessness. Otherwise we won't work to get there." And 70-year-old Aaron Feuerstein who kept paying his loyal workers and keeping up their health insurance after his mill burned to the ground. A practicing Orthodox Jew, he seemed confused when he was called a "great American hero." He merely quoted our friend, Hillel: "When all is moral chaos, this is the time for you to be a *mensch,*" a just and caring human being.

Would it not be a worthy goal for each of us to aspire to be a *mensch?*

In these times, I do not believe there is an acceptable option. Remember, if it is not us ... who? For, after all, what brings us to this place, this church? Is it not a belief, or a wish to believe, that there is something, some force, some truth, that is larger than we are? Is it not a hope that the human spirit can soar on the wings of decency and compassion? The hope, as metaphoric as it may be, that a godlike something wants us to do better, to be better? For, what is the value of our sentience, our consciousness, if not to rise to higher levels of goodness?

Perhaps you even share my vision that, if there is a Supreme Being, and if we should appear before that being for judgment, we would be asked only one, simple question: "How did you treat other people?"

Let our leaders answer for themselves. As for us, there is a way to prepare: The old Hebrew admonition to live each day as if the Messiah were coming tomorrow.

Finally, we must ask ourselves: have all the wars and cruelties and inquisitions and holocausts and slaveries taught us nothing? Will America, this two-century-old experiment in government by the people turn to ashes, the victim of greed and scapegoating of the downtrodden.

The Kotzker Rebbe, a Jewish wise man and teacher, said: "Take care of your own soul and another person's body, not of your own body and another person's soul."

We are, after all, not admonished to be our brother's judge or our sister's oppressor. We are taught to be their keeper. Let us, for God's sake, get about that task . . . now.

My America

Sudden End for a Time of Hope

I t was early on a Sunday morning—about 7 o'clock—as I tooled my white Rambler up Capitol Hill. I turned into the garage under the Old Senate Office Building, parking in my boss's space. Sen. Tom McIntyre wouldn't be in today, and not just because it was Sunday.

Capitol police had stopped me twice even before I reached the garage and again at the elevator and outside the office door. Armed National Guardsmen lined the streets and the majestic steps of the Capitol itself.

"Too late," I told myself, and began sobbing, as I had on and off since Friday. Could it have been only two days since it had happened? Could I feel so much older in so short a time? Could a world full of hope be plunged into darkness by a few bullets fired from a cheap rifle in Dallas?

But I put aside those questions. Sen. McIntyre had directed me to write a newsletter to the people back home in New Hampshire about the terrible event. Our offices were empty, and the light was gray. I turned on my desk lamp, sat down, rolled a piece of paper into my typewriter and stared at it. After a while, the silence was broken as I began to type:

"'The New Frontier is in New Hampshire just as much as it is in Alaska, just as much as it is in any section of the world.' Thus spoke John Fitzgerald Kennedy in Manchester, September 2, 1960."

It was just two months after that speech that I first saw John Kennedy in person. I was a newsman for The Associated Press, one of a team assigned to cover Sen. Kennedy's speech in a park across the street from the Union Leader newspaper offices in Manchester.

It was November 7, the night before the election, and it was no surprise that Kennedy had come at the last minute to a small state he was assured of winning. William Loeb, the poison-tongued publisher of the Union Leader, hated the Kennedys and had, of late, been particularly vicious in attacking Bobby Kennedy. Jack Kennedy was in New Hampshire to fire a last-minute salvo across the bow of the right-wing publisher. And he did. He told a screaming throng of partisans on that chill Monday evening:

"I would like to have the Union Leader print a headline that we carried New Hampshire. I believe there is probably a more irresponsible newspaper in the United States, but I cannot think of it. I believe that there is a publisher who has less regard for the truth than William Loeb, but I cannot think of his name."

I tried my damnedest to maintain my reportorial objectivity and skepticism, but it was no good. I was spellbound. It was the last thing I expected. I was not a Kennedy fanatic; he did not seem liberal enough for me. I had still cherished the hope—now dashed—that Adlai Stevenson might pull off a miracle and win the Democratic nomination in 1960. Of course, I supported Kennedy, but then I probably would have voted for the devil incarnate against Richard Nixon, a man I had detested since my teens.

But on that autumn night I listened to a man exuding hope and confidence, a man unafraid to call upon Americans to sacrifice to insure the future, just as those before us had sacrificed. John Kennedy, to use a word currently in vogue, empowered us—not to get a condo and a Mercedes, but to work for a brighter future for everyone. I was sold.

Still, there was no way to tell that night that almost exactly two years later, I would be driving from New Hampshire to Washington, DC, having tossed aside a 13-year career in journalism to participate in the excitement of the Kennedy era. Nor could I guess that only a year after my arrival, the young leader would be dead.

For many of us still in our early years (I was 32), when the eternal flame was lit above JFK's grave, another flame, signifying a kind of American innocence, was extinguished.

I continued typing:

"To John Kennedy the New Frontier was a thing of the mind rather than of geography. These frontiers were in a new dimension. They were not to be gained, as those of our forefathers, by traveling West in a covered wagon. They were of the mind, the heart, the spirit, and were to be won with courage, determination and a deep desire that all people should live in peace and with dignity."

The revisionists have raped history and left us with the picture of a president with a giant libido and tiny accomplishments. Even with no clue that the gossips-cum-historians would later bury much of the truth beneath a layer of innuendo, I wrote that Kennedy gave us "something to excite the youth of the nation, to stimulate the talents of our people and give direction to an uncertain and faltering world. This idea burst like the light of the sun upon a nation and a world that had been dwarfed by the tiny atom and saw no new paths to glory."

Were there mistakes? Of course. The Bay of Pigs and sticking our toe into murky waters in Vietnam, to name a couple.

Was there uncertainty? This is an example some say is apocryphal, others swear is true. After relentlessly seeking the presidency for a decade, Kennedy finally was seated alone in the Oval Office for the first time. He called in his close friend and adviser, Kenneth O'Donnell. "Kenny," the president of the United States is alleged to have said, "what the fuck do we do now?"

But no accomplishment? There was the epochal partial ban on the testing of nuclear weapons. Does it seem inconsequential now, in the wake of the demise of Communism and the USSR? Well, at the time, when the nuclear clock was running out, it seemed a solid step away from oblivion. Remember, people were still digging fallout shelters in their backyards, and school kids were being taught to hide under their desks when the "big one" hit.

I will never forget standing in the corner of the US Senate floor when Sen. Clair Engle of California was carried in on a stretcher and a colleague held up his arm for him to vote for the treaty. Engle, dying of brain cancer, wished to make this his final Senate vote.

Did Kennedy move slowly on civil rights? By the light of later years, perhaps yes. But he was moving in the right direction when too many others were fighting any change. And when he learned the lessons (both moral and political) from Martin Luther King and others, he committed to the fight for equal rights.

This youngest of presidents was deeply concerned with making life more secure and dignified for the elderly, from housing to medical care. By creating the Peace Corps, he gave young people a place to exercise their altruism while erasing the picture of the Ugly American. Today we are told it is too expensive to allow our young people to lead us again in a direction away from selfishness and greed.

Perhaps as important as all the rest was Kennedy's vision of and concern about the rise of extremism. It is ironic that in a speech he never delivered in Dallas on November 22, 1963, Kennedy was to say:

"Today other voices are heard in the land—voices preaching doctrines wholly unrelated to reality, doctrines which apparently assume that words will suffice without weapons, that vituperation is a good as victory and that peace is a sign of weakness. . . . We can hope that fewer Americans will listen to nonsense."

So my newsletter concluded: "If John Kennedy's all-too-brief life and tragic death are to have any meaning, we must follow this clarion call. We must use the tools of liberty to crush the growing cancer of hate and doubt that is about this land. We must accept fully the inheritance of courage which John Kennedy has left us."

As I rolled the final sheet from the typewriter, my mind went back two days to Friday noon when Marty Smith, Sen. McIntyre's home-state assistant, picked me up at Logan Airport for a drive to New Hampshire.

At about 2 PM, we pulled into the garage where Marty had leased the car. It seemed strange that no two people in the garage were standing together; usually there were little knots of people talking and laughing.

"It's Kennedy." I heard someone say that first, and somehow I knew, even before I saw that he was wiping tears away with his sleeve. Marty and I got out of the car, and in a moment everyone gathered around us. "The president is dead." "Oh, my God. The bastards shot him."

I moved to the far side of the garage and didn't stop until I was alone, my face just inches from the cinder-block wall. There were no tears, just a low moan that seemed not to have come from me.

Later, in my hotel room, I felt compelled to return to Washington and be present at the rites. I called Governor John King's office and was assured a seat the next morning on the National Guard plane taking the Governor and his entourage to the funeral.

Saturday. I don't remember the time. There was a steady rain as I stood in line with Sen. and Mrs. McIntyre and Jim Keefe, the senator's top aide and my friend. An honor guard from each of the armed forces lined the White House drive, droplets of rain tracing down their faces. A crowd was gathered in Lafayette Park across the street from the White House. Some had umbrellas; others just stood, unmoving, soaked. There wasn't a sound.

We moved inside and slowly followed the line into the East Room. There on a black catafalque rested the flag-draped coffin; it was barely believable that inside lay the remains of the man who until 24 hours earlier had represented life and energy and hope to millions around the world.

The ornate chandeliers were draped in black. Huge candles burned near the corners of the coffin. Young honor guardsmen stood stiff, eyes fixed, praying they would not faint. On the wall behind the coffin were gold-framed portraits of George and Martha Washington.

I went home to a blur of television, trying to explain to my 5-year-old son, David, something I hardly believed, much less understood. My wife Dina and I tried conversation, but it didn't work. There was just the television.

Sunday. By the time I had finished writing the newsletter, Dina and Jim and Janet Keefe arrived at the office. We were to join the many thousands viewing the coffin, which by now had been transferred to the Rotunda of the Capitol. The body had been borne from the White House on the same caisson that had carried Franklin D. Roosevelt in 1945.

We made our way underground through a tunnel connecting the Senate office building to the Capitol. We stood at the edge of the giant circular area to listen to the speeches. Senate Majority Leader Mike Mansfield, a gentle man from Montana, repeated, over and over, in his address: "And she took the ring from her finger and placed it in his hand."

The sun shone through the clerestory windows atop the towering Capitol dome. The coffin now rested on the catafalque that was used for Abraham Lincoln a century earlier. It seemed tiny in this vast area, ringed with statues of the great and the now obscure. Exercising the small amount of authority we had, we were allowed to break into the line, and the four of us paused before the coffin. This time the tears came, and we held onto each other because there was nothing else to do.

Sometime during this day we learned that Lee Harvey Oswald had been shot and killed. It seemed to make things worse.

Monday. Another sunny day, a day for burial. Jim Keefe and I stood on the Capitol steps as the procession formed to go to the cemetery.

Besides the Kennedy family and friends, it was an occasion only for the high and mighty. Nonetheless, we were determined to go. Jim, his Irish charm at full throttle, was working on Senate Sergeant-At-Arms Joe Duke, who was in charge of the procession and in no mood for a chat.

We were about to give up, our hands thrust deep in our overcoat pockets, our heads bent, when Duke said, "Okay, dammit, get into that Army station wagon at the rear, and keep your damn mouths shut." The cortege moved ever so slowly. Mrs. Kennedy, the children, the family and the kings and princes were walking at the head of the procession.

The line wound its way past the Lincoln Memorial, across Memorial Bridge and through the gates into Arlington National Cemetery. By the time we made our way from the car to the gravesite, we could see the assemblage ringing the grassy slope. There were the famous and the powerful: de Gaulle from France, Haile Selassie from Ethiopia, Prince Philip of England, Mikoyan of the USSR. The family was blank-faced, exhausted. The members of the Irish Mafia, that coterie of friends who were with Jack from Day One, looked lost.

Saddest looking was Richard Cardinal Cushing of the Archdiocese of Boston. He had married Jack and Jackie, blessed John John and Caroline, buried little Patrick Bouvier. He had given the prayer at the inauguration a thousand days before as the nation's first Catholic president took office.

I found a small space next to Sen. Edmund Muskie of Maine, a long-time friend of the president, as Cardinal Cushing intoned the ancient Latin words in a flat, Boston monotone. Some of his words were drowned out as a flight of Air Force jets, with an empty place in the formation honoring the fallen commander-in-chief, roared overhead.

Deep-voiced cannons thundered a 21-gun salute. Riflemen fired three volleys. Taps sounded and echoed in the distance. The triangular-folded flag was handed to the widow. The eternal flame was lit. We repeated the Lord's prayer, and it was over.

Again?

"**K**ennedy's dead. He was shot." I sat bolt upright in bed, wakened from a deep sleep by the words on the telephone from my old friend, Jack Teehan.

"Oh, my God," I whispered to no one, "the President's dead." As I hung up the phone without finishing the conversation, I saw by the luminous dial on the clock that it was 3 A.M. I swung out of bed noiselessly so as not to wake my wife, and as I gained conscious thought, I realized that it was June of 1968, and the President had been dead almost five years.

What the hell had Jack been talking about? I knew that he often sat up far into the night, sipping Scotch, and sometimes calling me at ungodly hours with all manner of stories. But, just in case, I went downstairs and switched on the television. In those days there was little all-night programming, unless some extraordinary news story occurred. As the screen lit up, I could see there was something going on.

In a minute, I knew that Jack was right. Kennedy had been shot. Kennedy was dead. Robert Kennedy. As I sat there, alone, it was almost too much to bear: the image of another national leader, his young life bleeding out of him. Bobbie lying quietly, almost peacefully on the worn floor near a back entrance he was taking for safety—bending over him in disbelief the hulking form of his friend and protector, football great Rosie Greer.

A friend of mine told me that Camelot and all its promise ended the moment Sirhan Sirhan squeezed the trigger and killed Bobbie, who dreamed of things the way they could be and said "why not?"

"I can't stand it," I said aloud, immediately feeling guilty for such a selfish thought. But it was understandable, especially for folks—like me—who had been living and working in Washington during the first half of the '60s, when assassination had become almost commonplace.

It was just two months earlier when the national psyche had been torn apart once again. Along with several hundred other Democratic Party loyalists, I was attending a gala political banquet in the District of

Columbia, highlighted by the attendance of both President Johnson and Vice President Humphrey. Halfway through the chicken dinner, the Master of Ceremonies, Senator Edmund Muskie of Maine, was called away from the head table. He returned somber-faced with an announcement I recall this way:

"Ladies and gentlemen, I have a sad announcement. Martin Luther King Jr. has been shot. We don't have details, but we fear there may be trouble in the streets. Let us stand for a moment of silent prayer, and then please file out quietly and go to your homes."

It was dark as my friend, Jim Keefe and I headed back to our homes in the white suburbs of Maryland. Without thought we took our usual route home, smack through the black ghetto. "Jesus," Jim said, "I need gas." We stopped at the first station, where the black owner pumped just a few gallons and then said "You guys better get the hell out of here now."

As we looked around, we saw knots of people gathering together in the streets. As Jim tooled the Mustang back onto the main street, a wave of fear shot through me—the kind of fear black people must experience even today when, innocent of wrongdoing, they are stopped as they drive through white neighborhoods late at night.

The murder of Bobbie Kennedy in California pulled my mind back to the Lorraine Hotel balcony in Memphis, where King was killed and to Dealey Plaza in Dallas where JFK's life and promise ended in a moment of disbelief. For my generation, and perhaps others to come, it was the murder of hope. It was the time when a belief in sacrifice for the greater good turned first to despair and then to skepticism and, by now, a widespread cynicism and egocentrism.

Viewed through the prism of today's sensibilities, or lack of same, it was not difficult to understand the anger and bitterness of some pundits and many writers of letters to the editor about the attention given to the death of the President's son, and the funds expended on the retrieval of his body and aircraft from the Atlantic off Cape Cod.

There are at least two ways of looking at this phenomenon. First, there is the obsessive cult of celebrity, mirrored through the various media, that stirs a kind of international madness and sadness over the death of celebrities—particularly young ones such as JFK Jr. and Princess Diana. (And, remember, JFK was just in his mid 40s, Robert only 42 and King 39 at the times of their deaths.) The laying of flowers and notes outside homes and the tears for the TV cameras perhaps reflect a need for connection with these famous people and, at the same time, a fear that if such vibrant and protected entities can be snatched away so easily, how safe from similar fates are we common folk.

But for me and, I would guess, a lot of my contemporaries, the death of JFK Jr. brought sad memory back to life. The tears I shed that week were not only for those three young people under the sea, but also for President Kennedy, Reverend King, Senator Kennedy. And me.

John Adams and I
Celebrate the Fourth

". . . I am well aware of the toll and blood and treasure that it will cost us to maintain this Declaration and support and defend these states. Yet through all the gloom, I can see the rays of ravishing light and glory. I can see that the end is more than worth all the means. And that posterity will triumph in that day's transaction, even though we should rue it, which I trust in God we shall not."

(Excerpt from a letter from John Adams to Abigail Adams,
Philadelphia, July 3, 1776)

On reading that letter, one cannot but wonder were President Adams here today, would he rue the day that he and the other founders signed the Declaration of Independence, in an act of courage, daring and foresight perhaps unequalled in history's pursuit of human dignity and liberty.

Or would he find, as he prayed on that scorching hot day in Philadelphia, that their labors had brought forth light and glory and triumph?

How would he have measured the words that long-ago year published by pamphleteer Tom Paine—"These are the times that try men's souls . . . .Tyranny, like hell, is not easily conquered."—against the fulminations and shallow sound bites that today fill the airwaves and the halls of Congress?

How might Adams have rated today's cold-hearted leaders who attack the poor, the weak, the old and the disabled in a cowardly and mindless blood game for power and money against his colleagues who pledged "our lives, our fortunes, and our sacred honor" in what they knew was a bloody war to come against a tyrannical autocrat?

One must exercise care not to answer questions such as these too facilely or with too much hubris. And so I thought about all the things I did on this July 4th, and wondered how those events might have differed had I been accompanied by Mr. Adams, our neighbor from

Quincy, Mass. How might this founder of our nation have thought of an Independence Day in a United States unlike one he could have imagined?

I began the day, as usual, with breakfast and newspapers. One journal, as was its habit, published the Declaration of Independence as its editorial. I read it over twice and underlined the following passages:

". . . governments are instituted among Men, deriving their just powers from the consent of the governed."

". . . governments long established should not be changed for light and transient causes . . ."

"He (King George III) has endeavored to prevent the population of these States, for that purpose obstructing the laws for naturalization of foreigners, refusing to pass others to encourage their migration hither . . ."

Reading further in the newspapers one got a modern-day up-dating of the founder's immortal words. For example, the words of the majority leader of the US House of Representatives, Dick Armey of Texas. When speaking of the career chosen by Adams and Jefferson and himself, he said "the market is rational and the government is dumb." And also the latest diatribes demanding we sever relationships with NATO, the UN and other alliances that slow a move toward total isolationism and xenophobia.

Oh yes, five candidates for president announced proudly that they had amassed more than $22 million in just three months, as though this was some measure of their ability to govern instead of a more plausible scenario—auctioning off their political souls.

Still another story told of the surge in interest in the campaign of one Patrick Buchanan, all echoes of his racism, anti-Semitism, xenophobia and homophobia muted in a kinder and gentler Buchanan-speak and forgotten by the media. A new and improved candidate who no longer talks of the "genius" of Hitler, his affection for Franco or his belief that AIDS is a kind of divine punishment on erring human beings.

Mr. Adams, who had been reading over my shoulder, whispered "so much for our lives, our fortunes and our sacred honor."

Next, after I explained to him what television was, Mr. Adams and I watched the movie of John Steinbeck's masterwork, *The Grapes of Wrath*. It tells the story of the exodus of a group of destitute farmers from Oklahoma to the promised land in California after unrelenting winds had turned their land into a dustbowl. The Joad family makes the trek along Route 66 in a ramshackle truck overloaded with their poor goods and needy friends.

Along the way, Grandpa Joad dies and is buried beside a desert road. The preacher they have carried along the way, disillusioned and having forgotten all his prayers, says simply "all that lives is holy."

Later, used, abused, beaten and cheated in California's picking fields, Henry Fonda, as oldest son, Tom Joad, preparing to run from police, says to his mother: "Maw, they're workin' on our spirit, our decency."

I told Mr. Adams of Cesar Chavez, a real man who died too young 60 years later fighting the same battles. Mr. Adams sniffed, wiped the corners of his eyes with a lace handkerchief but would admit only to "a small illness of the nasal passages."

"But wait," Mr. Adams said to me as we headed out to lunch; "Is there nothing to read this Independence Day to make me feel that our work left its mark?"

I searched further and found a story that said "two lonely liberals" had blocked Senate approval of cuts in programs to provide heating assistance to the poor, train the jobless and other social programs. The story said Senators Paul Wellstone and Carol Mosely-Braun "parted company" with President Clinton and senior members of their own Democratic Party as well as Republicans to make their stand.

"Now my appetite is rising," Mr. Adams said. "Tell me a word or two about these legislators."

"Mr. President," I replied, "your seeds have borne fruit. The one is a black woman who has risen by her own efforts in a political world still dominated by white men, and the other is a Jewish college professor from the mid-West."

"This was beyond even my dreams, but not beyond my understanding or approval," he said.

A half-hour later, Mr. Adams and I were seated in a Chinese restaurant with my 91-year-old mother who was explaining to the President the finer points of choosing between moo goo gai pan and chicken lo mein.

Now he turned to my mother, who was born just 78 years after his death, and said "Tell me, Sophia, what was America like when you were young? Did our labors bring any light and glory into your life? Did you celebrate Independence Day?"

Leaning back in her wheel chair and exercising the familiarity earned by the old, she said, "Well, John, my life has spanned the best and worst of times. I remember my early Independence Days as we approached World War I. In late afternoon, the family would gather— uncles and aunts and first cousins, some 30 of them—and walk up to Ferry Street to get on the old open-sided street car and ride to Glendale Park for fireworks.

"First there were speeches by the local political and business leaders, orations and readings from your Declaration, John. Just when we kids thought we would die from boredom and explode with anticipation, the fireworks would start. The showers of colored sparks, the echoing explosions, and everybody waving little American flags and singing patriotic songs.

"Later, of course, John, I lived through two world wars, one giant depression, a bout with near-poverty and the death of just about everybody I loved from my generation. But I love and believe in America, John, and have high hopes for my great granddaughter, Sarah. She might even be president some day."

Later that afternoon, Dina and I headed down to our son David's new house for a Fourth of July cookout and fireworks. Noticing Dina's accent, Mr. Adams asked her how long she had been in this country, and what brought her here.

"I came to this country in 1950, Mr. President," she said, explaining to him how she was caught in the Holocaust and endured Auschwitz. Her story was punctuated by Mr. Adam's exclamation—"Oh, Lord," and "I can't imagine." But he brightened up along with her as she reminisced about the day she became an American citizen.

"My father and I decided we would be naturalized together. We studied, and I questioned him about the presidents, including you, about your Declaration, and the Constitution and Bill of Rights. It was harder for him, he was already in his 50s and English was a new language. But he wanted so much to be an American.

"From the time we arrived at New York, my dad told all six of his children that we were to speak only English to him. Then the day came. I put on my best dress and the orchid Norman brought to me; Daddy was handsome in his navy suit and starched white shirt.

"We gathered at the Federal courthouse in Concord, where the oath of citizenship was administered by Judge Connor. As we recited the Pledge of Allegiance, I thought what a long way I had come from a small Polish village by way of Auschwitz to be free again in America. Thank you, Mr. Adams. Thank you for the United States."

Mr. Adams enjoyed the cookout at David's home, but we couldn't get him to go into the pool. He was fond of the hot dogs and potato salad. "Delectable," he said.

On the way home, Mr. Adams said his time was up, and asked to be let out at the roadside.

"May I leave you with a couple of quotes, Mr. Adams, that might have come from your lips?" I asked.

"A professor of political science, Benjamin Barber, told an audience in the former Communist Czech Republic, that 'democracy is a process, not an end; an ongoing experiment not a set of fixed doctrines.... When a nation announces the work of democracy finished, it's usually democracy that is finished in that nation.'

"At the same time, Czech President Vaclav Havel was telling an American audience, Mr. Adams, that serving the community was 'morality in practice.' And he added that 'The main task of the coming era is a radical renewal of our sense of responsibility.'"

"It's just as I wrote Abigail in that letter in 1776," President Adams replied, "I can see the rays of ravishing light and glory."

Then he was gone.

LBJ: Up Close and Personal

The door opened and in wiggled two beagles on a double leash. Everyone in the Fish Room at the White House jumped out of his seat and stood at the bureaucratic equivalent of attention.

We all knew that holding the other end of the leash was the owner of Him and Her, a man who was known notoriously for having hoisted the dogs up by the ears to the delectation of press photographers and the horror of the ASPCA.

But on this Saturday morning, we were wondering why President Lyndon B. Johnson was wandering into a middle-level meeting, and, more importantly, what he wanted.

"Sit down, fellas," he said as he pulled a chair out from the table and arranged his anything-but-svelte form, stretching his long legs half-way across the room it seemed. Johnson was wearing a tan western shirt, open at the collar, gray flannel slacks with a razor-sharp crease, and cordovan loafers buffed to a high sheen.

Larry O'Brien, the former JFK top aide who had made the transition to Johnson's staff, was running the meeting at which we were reporting our vote counts after lobbying members of Congress on key Johnson legislation for low-income housing. "Would you like us to give our reports to you, Mr. President?" O'Brien asked.

"Shit no, Larry," the leader of the free world answered. "I'm just lonesome. Lady Bird's off somewhere, and I'm looking for company. Just go right on."

A palpable nervousness ran through the room. What had been a relaxed meeting among approximate equals, suddenly was show-and-tell at the highest level. The President was not a man known for patience and equanimity; and he damn sure didn't suffer fools with any gladness at all, as we were soon to find out first-hand.

I was at the session as back-up for my boss, Bernie Boutin, the Democratic activist who had held several high-level appointments under both Presidents Kennedy and Johnson. At this time, Bernie was in the private sector as executive vice-president of the National Association of Home Builders. I was also there as a lobbyist, and was doing part of the vote gathering for LBJ's legislation.

If I was nervous just being at a White House meeting, my blood pressure soared after the President came in. What if he asked me a question that I couldn't answer, I thought irrationally, not realizing that he didn't have a clue who I was and was the last person he'd seek information from.

As the meeting went on, conversation turned to the relationship between low-income housing and civil rights. One of the second-level Cabinet members, either to apple-polish or innocently, asked: "Mr. President, how did a person like you, born and raised in the southwest, develop such a sensitivity for minorities?"

The President looked the hapless questioner right in the eye and said: "Who the fuck do ya think I played with on the Perdenales River when I was a kid? Black kids. Brown kids. And I was as goddam poor as they were."

After a few moments of dead silence, the meeting went on—and on and on. Some of the Ivy League-bred officials around the table were ensconced in intellectual nit-picking when Johnson interrupted to ask how many people around the table had ever run for office.

"I know the answer," Johnson said. "Me and Bernie Boutin are the only sumabitches in this room. Bernie was mayor of Laconia, New Hampshire, and he learned the way you get things to happen is to know the people and talk to them in their language, not with a bunch of high-level crap."

Johnson went on to order all present to attend a barbecue the following week which Bernie and Alice Boutin were to put on at their home in Virginia. Boutin was ordered to give the Cabinet officials a primer on running for local office. I don't think the event ever took place, but I was one proud guy to be working with a man who was admired as much by LBJ as he had been by JFK.

The pride only swelled when, at the conclusion of the meeting, my turn came to shake hands with the President and tell him for whom I worked.

"You're damn lucky," he said, as I craned my neck up toward his face. "You listen to what Bernie says, and you'll go a long way."

The Party's Over

have ended my lifelong membership in the Democratic Party.

First, I wrote a letter to the state headquarters of the Democrats, stating my intention. Then I went to the office of the city clerk and had the "D" excised from after my name on the voting lists.

To understand fully the gravity and import of this decision, one would have to know that in my family, for the three generations they have been in this country, being a Democrat has been an article of faith. In my parents' house in Massachusetts, discussions around the kitchen table were almost always about politics, and almost never carried on in anything less than a full-throated yell.

The house was a meeting place and haven for Democratic office-holders and hangers-on. My father's weekly poker games would include such as Lt. Gov. Bob Murphy, members of Congress and the state legislature. The first celebrity I ever met—I was so young she lifted me onto her lap—was Frances Perkins, Franklin D. Roosevelt's secretary of labor and the first woman Cabinet member.

We were working class, pro-labor, anti-big business and adorers of FDR and Harry Truman. In my family, the only election year choices we made were in the Democratic primary; in the general election, it was easy: just put an "x" in the circle for voting a straight Democratic ticket.

You could always tell election times because my mother's bridge table would be moved next to the telephone, groaning under the weight of lists of voters waiting to be called. I started working the polls before my tenth birthday.

My dad walked the three-deckers in Brighton for John Kennedy the first time he ran for Congress, and with Tip O'Neill when he, later, ran for the same seat. I spent seven years in Washington in the 1960s on the staff of Sen. Tom McIntyre of New Hampshire and in the Executive Branch under Presidents Kennedy and Johnson.

But in the 43 years since I came to New Hampshire, there had been only five successful candidates for high office with a "D" after their names I was able to vote for.

Historically, only about one in ten New Hampshire governors has been a Democrat, and Democrats have not controlled the Legislature since Civil War times.

Is this sorry record because Democrats always put up terrible candidates while the Republicans field only latter-day Teddy Roosevelts? Absolutely not. Some darn good people have run as Democrats. And pedestrian would be a good word to describe a lot of recent GOP office-holders; in a real two-party state, many of them would have chosen other lines of work.

Now, before the charges of traitor start coming my way, let me explain why I made my decision. The Democratic Party is disorganized and disheartened. It has become too much a party of exclusion, of single-issue folks with an abiding interest in their issue and nobody else's. A lot of good workers are ignored or patronized. There seems little room to disagree or try to have input to the leadership circles. There is little candidate-building or encouragement of new strategists from outside the circle.

What message there is, is muddled, and there is a fear to challenge the opposition with real problems, to demand positive performance from elected officials. The Democrats seem always to be playing in the other guy's ball-field instead of establishing goals to educate the electorate on how they are being taken for a ride by the Republicans. Sure, there are some good people working very hard inside the party, but in politics the name of the game is to win without losing your honor.

Adlai Stevenson once said "The hardest thing about any political campaign is how to win without proving that you are unworthy of winning."

On the other hand, Sen. Tom Harkin, a real Democrat, said "the only thing the American people like less than a dirty fighter is someone who won't fight." The Democratic Party both locally and nationally is spending a lot of time proving the truth of both sentiments.

The real message of the sad slide of the Democratic Party is the contribution it made to the rise of Pat Buchanan and others in the hard right, as spokesmen for the working class in America. The Democratic

Party, skidding to the right, politically correct and awash in chablis and self absorption, abandoned its historic constituency and presided over the dissolution of its success-breeding coalition of working class, minorities, labor, the poor, mainstream religion, immigrants and young idealists.

It left lunch-bucket liberals like me and middle-aged, middle-class folks feeling like outsiders and politically incorrect slobs. The buttoned-up lawyers who were taught that wealth and winning are the highest values, and the political gurus with no allegiance to political party or ethical standards took over the party and ripped a giant hole in the fabric that held it together.

My grandfather, a labor union organizer, taught me, "Don't ever cross the picket line, son. Don't be a scab, because you'll be taking the food off another man's table. And someday, if we don't stand together, someone will take your job."

Well, my grandfather's concerns have come to pass. We haven't stood together, and Pat Buchanan and what he stands for have become the haven for the working class.

I've been a team player for more than four decades, voting straight party tickets, giving what money I could, working in a lot of campaigns, most often as a volunteer. When my non-Democratic friends have taunted me as a loser, I've talked proudly of standing by the principles of the Democratic Party, the party of the little person, the middle class, the down-and-outers, the party of labor unions and decent wages.

Well, they no longer are, and I've had enough, more than enough.

And while I'm no longer officially a member of the Democratic Party, I like to think I'll always be a Democrat. I hope that somewhere out there in the ether, my father and grandfather, who taught me politics, will understand.

America the Beautiful?

The big news dominated the New Hampshire media: It was opening day of the filling period for the 1996 first-in-the-nation presidential primary. In Concord, Patrick Buchanan, oozing his usual smugness and self-satisfaction, made news by being the first to sign on as a presidential candidate. In Manchester James Carville, a portrait of cuteness and self-promotion, made news merely by his presence as Democrats opened President Clinton's campaign headquarters.

In Washington and many of the state capitals, the war of attrition against America's helpless poor children, fueled by hatred and vindictiveness, continued unabated.

On that day "America the Beautiful" was being sung at lodge breakfasts and school assemblies across the nation. God's grace was sought to "crown our good with brotherhood from sea to shining sea." But neither our "good" nor our "brotherhood" seems evident to American children starving and hungry by the millions; children freezing in rat-infested hovels; children dying in stinking, crowded emergency rooms in crumbling ghetto hospitals. In other words, it was business as usual except in the huge field house at the University of New Hampshire at Durham. There, amid the scoreboards and team pennants, some thousand people sat mesmerized, for well over an hour. A small, spare man with a heart that seemed broken and a determination of steel, told us about the 48,000 human beings who spend their lives in a hell on earth called Mott Haven.

It is just nine stops and 18 minutes on Train Number 6 from the posh environs of the seventh-wealthiest congressional district in America to Mott Haven in the South Bronx, the poorest neighborhood in the poorest congressional district in the nation.

Jonathan Kozol had completed another of his books on the suffering of America's poor kids. Called *Amazing Grace: The Lives of Children and the Conscience of a Nation*, it is about Mott Haven, its children, and the ungodly lives we all are responsible in some measure for inflicting upon them.

Listening to Kozol, one must conclude that the conscience of America is nearly as dead as all the victims of AIDS and bullets and disease and starvation in Mott Haven. Kozol, who spent numberless hours among this subjects, his "good friends" he called them, does not look well. His face is drawn, and there is a sadness deep in his eyes, even when he laughs. Kozol contracted asthma during his days in Mott Haven, a disease he shares with many of the residents. He believes the sickness comes from inhaling the ashes of toxic medical waste, which is transported into the ghetto's incinerator from "rich" hospitals and clinics. "This is real refuse," he says angrily. "Limbs and organs and blood-soaked rags."

Kozol is a Harvard graduate and a Rhodes scholar who became a teacher in a poor black neighborhood of Boston. Over the past 30 years, he has written eight acclaimed books on education and social justice—or the lack of it—in the United States. But make no mistake, he is neither an academic lecturer nor a collector of data and charts. He is a witness and storyteller.

Kozol moves closely into the lives of America's throwaway children and their loving caregivers. He tells us how remarkable they are, dodging bullets, eating dry oatmeal and discussing Poe and the possibilities of heaven. It is clear he loves these kids, and believes them to be the helpless victims of our greed, bigotry and callousness. Of these children and their loving mothers and grandmothers, he fairly shouts, over and over: "They are innocent. They have done nothing wrong."

If you were to describe your neighborhood, how different would it be from Mott Haven? Two-thirds Hispanic and one-third black, the neighborhood has a median family income of $7,600 a year. At the elementary school only seven out of 800 students do not qualify for free lunch. Nearly one in four women tested in obstetric wards is HIV positive, and so the rates of AIDS babies are enormously high. Depression in children is common as are, increasingly, asthma and tuberculosis. The houses in the district, two-thirds of them city-owned, are freezing in the winter, sweltering in the summer, and rat-infested year-round. In 1991, 85 murders took place in the several blocks that make up Mott Haven.

Kozol tells his audience the stories of a few of his friends:

- Alice Washington, a 50-year old grandmother, has AIDS. While she is slowly dying, she is preoccupied with Kozol's safety and bad eating habits. She tells him of two hospital experiences she says are not unusual in her neighborhood. Stricken with pneumonia, she spent two days and two nights sitting in a chair in an emergency room, waiting for a bed. She sat among "sick children vomiting up their food. Old people coughing up their blood. Men with gunshot wounds. On the third day I gave up and went home." A second time, when she was told a bed was finally available, the bed was "covered with blood and bandages from someone else . . ." Her son wandered the hospital corridors, finding clean linen and washing down the bed.

  Mrs. Washington is a high school and secretarial school graduate who held steady jobs for more than 20 years until she was infected with AIDS by her supposedly monogamous husband. From there her life went downhill—three years with her kids in fetid homeless hotels in Manhattan until she was moved to the death trap of Mott Haven. Her son, David, tells Kozol one night: "Evil exists. I believe that what the rich have done to the poor in this city is something a preacher would call evil."

- The Rev. Martha Overall, a white Harvard graduate was well on her way to a rich and brilliant career in the law, when she had a transforming experience with the death of her younger brother to AIDS. She became an Episcopal priest and asked that she be sent to the poorest church in the poorest neighborhood. That is St. Ann's, smack in the middle of Mott Haven. Her life has become fused with the despised and blameless kids of the neighborhood, whom she offers food, time and non-judgmental love. Kozol raises her as a paradigm to those who ask "What can one person do?"

- An unidentified "rich friend." Kozol tells the audience that because of his long experience living among the hungry and the starving, he has a difficult time eating heartily. So when this friend invites Kozol to lunch at the posh Four Seasons, he declines, knowing two meals there exceed the dollars Mrs. Washington has for her entire family for a month. The friend presses him, worrying that he is malnourished, and Kozol relents. With the $100 lunch in front of him, uneaten, Kozol tells us: "As I looked at this man with his $80 shirt, his $3,000 Armani suit, his $20,000 wristwatch, his beautiful tan from a recent trip to the islands, I heard him complain—'Jonathan, we can't keep pouring money in. They're killing me with taxes. They're killing me'."

A recent reviewer said: "There must be something special about Kozol—a warmth, a gentleness, a kind of mournful decency—that brings out the extraordinary in others." These things Kozol certainly showed to the hushed audience, but he sent other messages, as well. I felt his horror, anger and despair that so many of us in this blessed nation could allow these centers for the death and destruction of children to exist among us; that we would vote for leaders who not only approve of this evil but also accuse these hapless victims of being responsible for America's ills.

History has shown us that any society that closes its heart to the oppressed and needy, sooner or later falls. Kozol has pledged his life, literally, to keeping this situation before our eyes, in much the same way as Martin Luther King, Jr. and Elie Weisel.

Kozol said he is often asked why he doesn't put a list of "things to do" at the end of his books. He makes it clear that if we still need such a list, it is too late, much too late.

It's the Act that Counts

D r. Martin Luther King Jr. lived only 39 years. What might he have further accomplished, where would his life have taken him, we might ask ourselves, had he not been martyred? He warned us on more than one occasion that he might not be with us all the way, but that we should carry on the battle without him.

Just four days after his assassination 29 years ago, the first King holiday bill was introduced in Congress. Since then, this nation and 49 states have enacted named King observances.

Less than a year after Dr. King's "I have a dream speech," Congress passed the seminal 1964 Civil Rights Bill. I had the great good fortune in those days to be an employee of the United States Senate, and to be among those on the team lead by Sen. Hubert Humphrey, working toward civil rights legislation. I also was among the quarter million people who marched and stood before the Lincoln Memorial that hot summer day, August 28, 1963, when Dr. King shook the nation awake with his dream.

I left the mall that day with a heart full of hope for an America that finally would fulfill its promise of justice and equal opportunity for all. Today I am less certain. But just because hope seems dimmer, is no reason to give up on the dream. Quite the opposite.

It is said in my religion, and probably yours, that the act is everything. That does not mean, of course, that words and ideas are unimportant, just that they are, by themselves, incomplete. For example, it is important to bring public attention to the fact that there are millions of hungry children in America. But once having knowledge, we have an obligation to act—to help get food to those kids.

Martin Luther King wrote and spoke about the injustices wrought upon his people. Better, perhaps, than anyone. But we know that he did not stop there. We know, for example, that while Doctor King's words were beginning to stir this nation, it was by an act of civil disobedience, and his resultant jailing, that he got the reluctant Kennedy administration to begin to respond actively.

For a number of years, I was involved (with some pretty wonderful people) in efforts to have New Hampshire enact a King holiday. I felt it was right and proper that my state should join the other 49 in marking Dr. King's achievements.

But while I applauded the efforts of those who chose to continue, I decided to do nothing further to promote an official King observance. No more of my energy would go into planning, scheming and cajoling to change what amounts to a racist attitude among some who had blocked the holiday.

In searching for a metaphor to explain my altered feelings, I remembered back when I was a young child and my momma tried to get me to eat rice pudding—a healthy and inexpensive dish in those post-Depression days. She told me how sweet it was. I kept my lips locked. She told me how nutritious it was. Still I wouldn't give in. She told me the rest of the family liked it. I was adamant. Finally, in exasperation, momma said she wasn't going to offer it to me anymore, because, with my closed attitude, I just didn't deserve it.

You know, it wasn't long after my mother stopped trying to force me to eat rice pudding that I tasted it. I liked it. Today, it's one of my favorites.

Martin Luther King's name and accomplishments already are woven securely into the fabric of this nation. It is pompous of us to think that we can do him further honor by arm-twisting reluctant dragons into grudgingly naming a day after him in our little state. But there is another way we can do honor to him—by carrying on his battle, working toward the full realization of his dream: feed the hungry; protect the little children; house the homeless; detest poverty, not the poor; end the tragic human flaw of color superiority; and fight for the rights of the oppressed and the downtrodden.

Dr. King told us on more than one occasion that he did not want to be remembered for his Nobel Prize or his many awards and honors. He said he wished to be recalled as a simple man who was a drum major in the march toward justice and equality. I believe he would tell us that in these mean and greedy times, when some of his accomplishments are being turned back, "Now don't all you bother with naming a day after me. You go out after those rich and powerful people in the board rooms and in the halls of Congress and the White House, and you tell them these words from Isaiah 3:13-15:

"It is you who have ravaged the vineyard; that which was robbed from the poor is in your houses. How dare you crush my people and grind the faces of the poor, says my God the eternal."

So we could do no greater honor to this man of destiny than by pledging—and acting on that pledge—to become foot soldiers in a parade toward a just and compassionate society. Marching behind the spirit of that drum major named Martin, and promising to continue the march until every living soul can proclaim in truth:

"Free at last! Free at last! Thank God almighty I'm free at last!"

N.H. became the fiftieth state to adopt a Martin Luther King, Jr. holiday

Kind Words Don't Fill the Belly

"**D**on't call that hungry, homeless child a spic." Does that sentence shock you? Is it intolerant? What about it is intolerant? If it is the use of the pejorative word "spic," then you are on the wrong track.

Too many of us in the liberal or progressive community are more concerned with calling someone an unacceptable name—and that word is certainly unacceptable—than we are with fighting those who are imposing unspeakably intolerant conditions, such as hunger and homelessness, on millions of innocent victims in our country.

We are increasingly intolerant toward those our religions tell us to help, those our Constitution orders us to treat equally, those to whom our very shared humanity should be screaming out: These are our children, our brothers and sisters. We must ease their pain.

Instead, we increasingly become more tolerant of the use of this very human misery as an excuse to disdain the needy. We, as a society, are hypocritically guilty of much of the intolerance for which we so piously condemn other societies. Poverty. Starvation. Homelessness. Racism. Child and forced labor. Xenophobia. Police brutality. Rape and incest. Allowing guns and drugs everywhere. Thievery and lying in high places in government and private industry. Withholding civil and human rights. And, most cowardly and duplicitous of all, blaming all of our ills upon the weak and powerless and downtrodden.

Intolerance, whether in family, community, workplace or in an entire nation, breeds mindless hatred and, perhaps even worse, insensitivity. After all, it's tough to live in the world's most affluent place where millions have no home and five million children don't have enough to eat—unless we de-humanize these people. The mean and weak men we have chosen to lead us know this, so they have chosen as our enemies the teenage black ghetto girl who gets pregnant, the indentured Chicano farm laborer, the white working poor, and the ever talked about, but rare, welfare queen.

They have made these unfortunate and powerless humans into symbols of sloth and evil. We are taught in many subtle ways they are inferior to us. In short, they have been de-humanized.

Be careful! This slippery slope of racial superiority and human degradation leads into a dark hole of hell. For it was this path, or ones like it, that made acceptable the enslavement of an entire black civilization and, later, the systematic slaughter of six million innocent humans, including 1.5 million children.

Meanwhile, how many of us are sitting by while these same lowlifes lead in the dismantling of the very institution which, for the past sixty years has shown a human face, a little compassion for the needy—the federal government? We are counseled that it takes a village to raise a child. Maybe. But it also takes commitment. And money. It takes the courage to say: "Yes, we will make it a high priority to feed hungry children, and find shelter for mentally ill people, and fund good schools for little black and brown kids so they'll have a chance."

Instead we are given code words like "ending welfare as we know it." How about ending child hunger as we know it. Homelessness as we know it. Racism as we know it. Corporate downsizing as we know it. $100 billion dollars a year in corporate welfare as we know it. An inexplicably bloated military budget as we know it.

Congress is talking about becoming more polite. To hell with politeness! I have no tolerance for it until it again provides formula and diapers to poor infants, until it puts rich and powerful crooks in the cell next to the ghetto kid who stole food for his family. Is it polite, or acceptable, that we eliminate all capital gains and inheritance taxes to aid the already rich, while 40 million people have no good access to health care? Is it polite to treat immigrants, mostly brown people, worse than we treat our dogs?

Why do we lionize the Trumps and the Perots for merely collecting money, while we desecrate the memories and belittle the good works of everybody from Martin Luther King, Jr. to Eleanor Roosevelt?

Why do we tolerate all of this? Do we really want to end poverty and discrimination and hunger and violence? Since we clearly have the laws and the resources—properly prioritized—to accomplish these ends, and since we are not doing so, I am afraid the answer is no. The answer is that we have neither the motivation nor the collective will to choose the obvious good over the spreading bad.

We are engaged in a class war in America. Our leaders, both public and private, have duped us into believing it is subversive to re-distribute wealth downward to the middle class and the needy, while they have successfully plotted unconscionable re-distribution upward to the few already dripping in under-taxed fortunes.

As we continue to close our eyes to this evil while vilifying the underclass, the cauldron of anger and frustration is coming to a boil. As the folk song says: "There's somethin comin', a great wave a runnin' to wash over all of us some soon day."

And, my friends, when that revolution comes, God help us all.

Justice for All?

There lives in this country, in this state, in this city, perhaps only blocks from that posh hotel across the street, a child, one beautiful, innocent child. She has a mind capable of learning, a body capable of growing strong and straight, a personality ready for fun and laughter and a good life.

But she is not learning. Her body is broomstick thin and beginning to bend. And she seldom laughs. Even at her tender age, she knows already that the good life is beyond her reach.

If we care to see why, we need only to look into the child's eyes. They are old eyes; eyes that have seen and know too much . . . too much for a child to have to bear.

Here is a not-so-unlikely future scenario if we continue on the present path:

Each morning the girl must get up for school, but how can she prepare properly? Her house is freezing cold, and there is no way to get it warm since the fuel assistance program has been abolished. There is a little food, but it must be saved for the evening meal, so she goes off in the chill winter air, hungry and wearing only a threadbare jacket. There are no dollars for warm clothes anymore since the state has been holding back block grant money from local welfare offices. School can do nothing more to fill the emptiness in the girl's stomach . . . the breakfast program is down the drain.

The little girl cannot understand why she is so poor, since both of her parents are working. What she doesn't know is that the minimum wage has been abolished and her hard working parents are paid the princely sum of $3 per hour, or $6,000 a year. That's about one-tenth the price of just one of the limousines that drove the nation's Republican governors to their conference here today.

What is perhaps worst is that too many of the people who govern us have stolen the dignity and self-worth of the little girl's mommy and daddy. They live with guilt and shame, at the lack of adequate food and clothes, and the pitifully poor gifts for their kids at birthday and

Christmas time.

The rich and the powerful who already own or control almost everything, seem to want it all . . . every last scrap. This bottomless greed is sucking the life out of the little girl and growing millions of others like her.

Incredibly, our leadership has chosen this little girl as the enemy. It is not the savings & loan thieves, or the Wall Street robbers, or the high-flying Washington lobbyists who have brought America low, we are told. It is not the bombers or ships that we do not need, not the thousand-dollar screwdrivers or five-hundred-dollar expense account lunches and posh vacations for Congressmen, we are assured. And of course it is not the tens of billions Congress shovels into the greedy maws of the conglomerates so they can advertise overseas with our dollars. Those things are okay.

But that damn welfare mother who cheats so she can feed her kids. She will bring America down, the patriots tell us. Well, it's time we put the blame squarely where it belongs. It is the shameless avarice of the rich and powerful that is weakening the republic. These are the locusts who are gobbling up the seed corn. These are the charlatans who are taking food from the mouths of poor children.

Enough!!

New York Supreme Court Judge Edwin Torres, a product of the East Harlem Barrio, once said these challenging words: "A society that loses its sense of outrage is doomed to extinction."

So I stand with you today in outrage. I join in your pain, your tears and your frustration . . . your sense of helplessness. But, my friends, none of these is enough. Our tears and our love and our sympathy will not put bread on the little girl's table, or clothe her, or provide honorable and decent paying work for her parents . . . it will do nothing to improve the quality of her miserable life.

No, finally, it is the act that is everything. And to us, and others like us, has fallen the task of acting. Let us accept this challenge, and take as our anthem the words spoken on the wintry day in 1961 in the nation's capital. The new president, John F. Kennedy, closed his inaugural address with these words: ". . . here on earth God's work must truly be our own."

I believe that in order to do that work we must, in the best sense, become radicals. Radical as were the ancient prophets. Radical as was Jesus, as was Mohammed. Radical like Abraham Lincoln and Franklin Roosevelt. Radical like Gandhi and Martin Luther King.

We must send a message to these steel-hearted tyrants that we will not be moved, that we will stand together upon the rock, that we will demand from them justice, decency, compassion, opportunity for every human being. That we will organize around these real family and human values. And that our numbers will grow. That we will no longer permit the people we elect and whose products we purchase to grow more and more wealthy and powerful at the expense of the poor and working people in this nation . . . our nation.

And when our numbers have multiplied, as surely they shall, we will shake the greedy and rapacious and comfortable down to their boots.

We will demand that the little girl never again feel hunger or be ill-clothed or cold, and we will make certain that she and her children are able to partake of the garden of opportunity that is now guarded by a sign reading: For the rich only.

And, further, we shall either break open their hearts of stone or cast out these cowardly bullies and haters and dividers.

And this nation shall make war no more upon the poor and the homeless, make war no more upon the helpless and destitute.

Instead we shall raise them up . . . we shall share gladly with them the bounty of this nation . . . we shall open to them the gates of our cities and the doors of our churches and synagogues and our mosques, and we shall—as our hearts dictate—call them brother and sister.

And, finally, we will raise our voices as one, in a thunderous roar and, in the words of the spiritual, declare:

> We shall not, we shall not be moved.
> We shall not, we shall not be moved.
> Just like a tree that's standing at the water . . .
> We . . . shall . . . not . . . be . . . moved.

Free Speech is Not Reserved for the Good Guys

The headline screeched "White Supremacists Shouted Down." About a dozen people, shouting sentiments I agree with in large part, prevented four people, whose beliefs I despise, from expressing those views on the State House Plaza on Monday—Martin Luther King, Jr. Day in all of America except New Hampshire.

New Hampshire Attorney General Jeffrey Howard, with one eye on the governor's office, expressed sentiments that shocked me more than anything either group espoused. Howard was quoted as saying: "The right to free speech is the right to speak—no one has the right to be listened to. It's the American way. If the voice isn't strong enough to drown others out, that's part of the free speech process."

Wrong, Mr. Howard. It's not part of the free-speech process when the protesters push over the white supremacist's podium. It's not part of the free-speech process when someone jams a crutch into the stomach of the white supremacist.

No, Mr. Howard, it is not part of the free-speech process when the state's top law enforcement officer says that might and superior numbers determine when free speech can be exercised.

Tell me, Mr. Attorney General, what would you do if I and others disrupted a State House Plaza speech by your patron, the governor, pushed over his speaking podium, shoved a stick into his stomach and shouted him down for four hours on state property? You're not suggesting, are you Mr. Attorney General, that freedom of speech is divisible, that it depends on who is seeking the right to exercise speech?

I am not opposed to demonstrations; I have participated in many. But I believe that if the cause is right, there is no need to silence the opposition. Quite the opposite, let the people hear the twisted and perverted views of the bigots and the haters. But if your cause is wrong, quieting the opposition will not work either.

As is so typical in much of the nation these days, the issues and the meaning of Martin Luther King, Jr. Day were lost in a welter of thoughtless shouting that marginalized the job ahead. Those of us who attended and participated in the many positive King observances Monday were reminded, more than anything else, that Dr. King's tasks remain unfinished, his dream only partially realized.

One-quarter of America's children live in poverty—the dream unfulfilled. Meanness is abroad in the land, compassion fading everywhere—the dream unfulfilled. Five black churches in one Tennessee city burned in just over a year—the dream unfulfilled. The nation turning its back on the needy, on education, on equal opportunity—the dream unfulfilled.

I hope that the protesters stayed to attend some of the King activities. Perhaps they could have learned a bit more about Dr. King's philosophy of peaceful, but forceful, resistance. I hope that Attorney General Jeffrey Howard attended a King event. Or if he was too busy, perhaps he took time to read through the entire First Amendment, which states not only that "Congress shall make no law . . . abridging the freedom of speech," but also guarantees the right of "the people peacefully to assemble. . . ."

But hope is, indeed, eternal. And I hope next year, I will not have to quote a white supremacist stating:

"It's interesting on the so-called Civil Rights Day, the civil rights people won't let me speak."

The Ice of Indifference

Thirty-five years ago, the government of the United States declared a war on poverty. In that same year, perhaps the single most compelling pieces of civil rights legislation in a century became the law of the land. Peace Corps volunteers from 18 to 80 had fanned out around the world to do good and bury the image of the Ugly American.

The Union of American Hebrew Congregations published a book, with a forward by Senator Hubert Humphrey, decrying poverty and hunger in America and pledging to join the effort to end these evils in the world's most affluent society. I am certain other religions did likewise.

Now, as we spin—largely out of control—into a new millennium, not only have those virtuous efforts been abandoned, they have also been tragically turned on their heads and made to seem shameful and useless and anti-American. In their place, we have declared a war on children, a war on the poor and homeless, a war on the helpless and hopeless in a once-compassionate society turned to stone.

Here are a few headlines to confirm that awful assertion:

- Republican leader declares war on social programs, says Great Society social programs "ruined the poor"
- Headstart to be cut
- Kids make up half of 27 million on food stamps; proposals made to cut feeding programs
- GOP Leader suggests orphanages for welfare kids
- Despite upturn, charities are hurting
- When schools close, kids go hungry

Finally, a quotation from a *Boston Herald* columnist: "Teens who have children out of wedlock have intentionally declared war on the rest of us. In self-defense, we must fight back."

Is there a connection between this heartless, mean-spirited attitude and the action of religion—particularly the regnant religious right? Or course. And it is governed by the new version of the Golden Rule: "Those who have the gold, rule."

Listen to this: At the opening of a posh Massachusetts shopping mall, a minister was enjoying a massage in a $3,000 "magic fingers" chair in a Brookstone's. He gleefully told a reporter: "Jesus said, 'I came that you may have new life—and have that life more abundantly.'" As he swung around in the chair and gestured toward the opulence surrounding him, he added: "And what do you suppose abundance means? All this, of course."

Now, as we swing around in the equivalents of the three-grand chair, as we get a tax cut, as the latest capital gains bonanza is on the way, as the savings and loan cheats walk the streets freely, having paid less than a penny on the dollar of their court-ordered fines, and as little girls in ghetto hellholes get pregnant as a way of creating someone to love—this once-compassionate society aims its millions of guns on the pitiful straw-man it has set up, the one cent on the tax dollar that goes for "welfare as we have known it."

"Ending welfare as we know it" is nothing more than code language for saying we will no longer make even a pretense for helping millions of hungry American kids or the growing ranks of mentally ill homeless or the too-soon-old ghetto kids. It is a signal that we fully intend, as public policy, to consign the least able and most helpless among us to the ash heap of expendability.

And it isn't only the cowardly bigots like Pat Buchanan and Pat Robertson or the oily hypocrites like Bill Bennett who peddle this chocolate-covered hate message.

The now-powerful religious right has winked its eye and given the politicians implicit permission to further damage the social contract that has been part of government and religion here since the beginning. This new class of "cut the weak and powerless loose" politicians knows it will be backed up by Robertson and Jerry Falwell and the million-member Christian Coalition.

But what of the remainder of American religion, the so-called mainstream?

It is pretty much off the radar screen—politically irrelevant. It has been timid, fractious, driven by single-issue politics, enchanted by political correctness. It has forgotten much of its core constituency, not in acts of charity, but rather in political leadership. It is not unlike the old bachelor uncle, cautiously wearing both belt and suspenders, who has all the right instincts but who is waiting for someone to lead and, in the meantime, feels vindicated because he has mailed a hundred bucks to the ACLU.

A man named Jim Wallis, who identifies himself as an evangelical Christian, in a book called *The Soul of Politics,* writes: "When politics loses its vision, and culture loses its soul—life becomes confused, cheap and endangered." He calls for a fusion of moral responsibility, which he says is the best impulse of conservatism, with "prophetic concern for social justice and change" best exemplified by liberals.

"This," writes Wallis, "would offer an alternative to the limits of secular humanism and the oppressions of religious fundamentalism." Wallis reminds liberals that in a society rife with racism, "merely to keep personally free of the taint of racist attitudes is both illusory and inadequate." He concludes that our divisions "are the defining story of the modern world."

Those of us who do not count ourselves among the religious right will continue to be politically irrelevant if, in the face of cutbacks in school feeding programs that help to keep 14 million kids from starving, we fight only against a moment of silence in schools. We will continue to be irrelevant if we fight only the battles of abortion, capital punishment and politically correct speech while the homeless are shut out of emergency shelters. And we may give up the right to call ourselves religious at all if we are complicit, by our silence if nothing else, in a government that blames poverty on the poor, homelessness on the homeless and senseless shootings on the ten-year-old who can get weapons as easily as bubble gum in a country obsessed with guns.

There is no need to repeat all the bad old quotes from Falwell, Weyrich and Robertson. But these people have moved darn close to their goal of what they call a Christian America. Only a fool could not have known their intentions or could have been surprised by their inexorable paths to victory.

I believe we know what must be done. We've got to get back in the game, and we've got to understand that we're playing on their field now.

As he was re-nominated for a second term more than 60 years ago, Franklin D. Roosevelt said these words: "The immortal Dante tells us that divine justice weighs the sins of the coldhearted and the sins of the warmhearted on different scales. Better the occasional faults of government that lives in a spirit of charity than the consistent omissions of a government frozen in the ice of its own indifference."

Translated into today's situation, the battle for the impact of religion and its teachings upon public life has been lost by those who favor a government living in the spirit of charity.

The war is not over, but it will no longer be sufficient for moderates and liberals, in and out of religion, to utter the institutional equivalent of "Don't you dare to call that starving, homeless kid a nigger." We must fight, and fight hard, for a government that hates hunger and poverty just as much as it hates hate language.

The future could well hinge upon our decision of whether and how deeply to get engaged—now.

"What Fools We Mortals Be"

I n mythology, the gods are immortal and have forever to make fools of themselves. We mortals are only around for an eye-blink in time and, thus, have to work fast.

I remember little else about the Shakespearean character, Puck, except that he said words to the effect: "What fools we mortals be."

One is moved to such lofty thoughts by the subterranean behavior of the mortals who occupy the Olympus of American public life, in general, and of the exquisite buffoonery we saw in the Clinton impeachment hearings and their run-up in specific.

"What does lying under oath do to the rule of the law?" asked the chair of the Judiciary Committee and erstwhile philanderer and fornicator, Henry Hyde. His ability to judge fellow-philanderer Bill Clinton in a fair and objective manner was untarnished, we are assured, because Hyde's affair happened as a youthful indiscretion—when he was in his 40s!

A heavy question for Chief Inquisitor, Kenneth Starr, came from California Congresswoman Mary Bono. Did he have animosity toward Chief Sinner Clinton? Nope, just doing his job. On another page of the same newspaper, Mary Bono went public with the news that the man she succeeded, late hubby and one-time Cher sidekick, Sonny, crashed to his death on a ski slope while he was heavy into prescription painkillers.

The huge hearing room was filled to capacity but, we are informed that just two of the seats are reserved for the "public." The line advances slowly as each pair of mortals has 30 minutes to breathe the heady air of Valhalla, while the remainder of the chairs are occupied, undoubtedly, by lobbyists and other greasers of the skids of government. All sit stern-faced for the TV cameras, but with visions of Monica and other sugarplum fairies dancing around in their heads.

One woman in line also attended the Watergate hearings. She calls the president a "moral moron," getting it just about right.

A young man heading for college said he was at the hearings

because he wanted to be president himself someday, that there's "no higher calling than public office, and I'm here to watch the system work." Could you make that up?

In the midst of all this making the system work, we were treated to the Monica-Linda audiotapes. Well, if we had any doubts about the serious intent of the prosecutor, the release of these tapes certainly is witness to his high purpose. Yeah, sure.

"Days Of Our Lives" and "General Hospital," at their best, couldn't hold a candle to the bathos of those conversations between a manipulative woman listening to tales of the intern, the president and a fine cigar.

Wait, there's more. How about this beaut of a quote from a White House source: "When people go to bed tonight, they'll be in the same place they were when they got up this morning." No wonder the dolt didn't want to be identified. Sen. Arlen Spector reached deep into his intellectual and philosophical core of wisdom: "I think the hearing will not change many minds."

Starr told the committee that Clinton carried out a "scheme to conceal" his affair. I guess Starr feels every public figure should stand up and confess to all their misdeeds, whether or not they're caught.

Hey, Ken, didn't you read the history books? Public confession would have wiped out, among many others, Washington, Jefferson, Franklin Roosevelt, John Kennedy, Eisenhower, Wilson, Reagan. Matter of fact, Mr. Starr, it would have left practically no one except the pure, like thee and me, and I have doubt about me. Starr, William Bennett and other self-appointed guardians of the moral behavior of the president—and you and me—would do well to heed these words from Edmund Burke, political philosopher: "Hypocrisy can afford to be magnificent in its promises; for never intending to go beyond promises, it costs nothing."

These purists railed on about the hard-to-define impeachment criteria of "high crimes and misdemeanors." Want a definition? How about 30 million hungry Americans, millions living on the streets, nearly 50 million with no access to health care, millions of working poor in dead-end, meaningless jobs, downgrading of the middle-class, a corrupt election system ruled by lobbyists for the rich, a media owned in large part by entertainment companies and conglomerates that is increasingly indistinguishable from the tabloid garbage spewers?

One doubts the frivolous pursuits of the media were what the Founders had in mind when they invented freedom of the press to keep the powerful and the rich on the straight and narrow. Nor, in my opinion, did the Founders, themselves escapees from religious/moral oppression, mean to find behavior such as Clinton's—scummy as it may be—to disqualify a man from presidency. But it is clear from other words they wrote and said that subverting or ignoring the rights and quality of life of any citizen, not setting as a goal "life, liberty and the pursuit of happiness" might well be grounds for disqualification.

And, in case you still don't believe we went over the edge in that whole seamy and childish episode in the history of a mighty republic, read this item, in its entirety, as published in *Nation* magazine:

> The FBI report on its interview with Monica Lewinsky describes the notorious cigar episode in clinical detail and then primly observes: 'The president did not smoke the cigar because smoking is forbidden in the White House.'

A Musical Awakening

mong the gifts I received this holiday season was a three-CD collection called "Women in Jazz." It features the incomparable voices of Sarah Vaughan, Billie Holiday, Ella Fitzgerald, Carmen McRae, Lena Horne and Dinah Washington.

I didn't play it right away; for a few days I savored the idea of it, fingering the box and reading the song titles. For some reason, I always practice delayed gratification with new books and music. Then one night, alone in my studio, I tore off the cellophane wrapper, put the discs into the machine and turned on the music.

Lady Day poured her heart out singing "God Bless the Child," "Lover Man" and "Do Nothin' Till You Hear From Me." Sassy Sarah trilled "It might As Well Be Spring" one minute and the next crooned smooth low notes in "The Nearness of You." Then Queen Ella and I danced "Cheek to Cheek," shared "Moonlight in Vermont" and, finally, tripped up a "Stairway to the Stars."

On the music spun, moving me—as jazz always does—to a different level of emotion and memory. This night the sounds carried me back half a century to another night, one that changed forever my way of listening and feeling.

The year was 1950. A 19-year-old hopeless romantic, my choice in music was limited to a pastiche of gloppy ballads, written, played and sung by white men and women for a monochromatic society. But all of that changed the evening Tobé, my then-girlfriend, persuaded me to go with her to the Hi-Hat, a night spot located in the heart of the black section of Boston.

It was the first time I had wandered beyond the comfort of the white world in which I lived and worked, so I was more than a little nervous and uncertain as we climbed the stairs to the second-floor lounge. About halfway up, I heard strange, new sounds—moving from ear-jolting discord to minor-key, bluesy sadness, to blasts of sheer jubilation. These riffs and hidden melody lines of jazz, improvised second by second, became over time both familiar and necessary pieces of my life. Like art, jazz asked nothing but to be allowed to enrich my life and broaden my understanding of the feats and foibles of us all.

That night at the Hi-Hat, we sat at a tiny round table no more than 15 feet from the bandstand. There, a young black musician in a beret, his cheeks puffed into balloons, took endless musical risks with dazzling speed. Yes, it was Dizzy Gillespie, and he showed me that night just how pain and joy really sound.

At the close of his set, and much to our pleasant surprise, Dizzy ambled over to our table and asked whether he could sit down. "I'll even bring my own booze," he added. With that, he slammed down a bottle that had a picture of a jungle cat and the words "Tiger Piss." It lived up to its name. I can't remember a word of our conversation, but I'll never forget that face, close up.

After that night, there was no need for Tobé to convince me to return to that stretch of Washington Street, where all the black jazz clubs were located. I became addicted to jazz and comfortable with my new intimate contact with black people. I grew used to the throat burn from cheap liquor, to the acrid smell of cigarette smoke mingled with the sweet aroma of smoke from those "other" cigarettes, which the musicians called reefer.

We went back, time after time, to that segregated enclave of black people and their music, mostly to the Hi-Hat and to a more "low-down" place called Wally's Paradise.

Our first time walking down the few steps to the entrance to Wally's, we hesitated inside the front door. It was a space not much larger than a couple of living rooms. There were about 30 black people in the audience, including a dozen sailors draped along the bar. Standing on a low platform was a lone musician playing "Sweet Georgia Brown" on the trumpet. When the song ended, Louis Armstrong spotted us and called out: "Come on in. Don't be 'fraid."

Well, thank heavens we did go in. Armstrong spun tune after tune, sang with that gravelly voice, marched between the tables, laughed and chatted. Maybe it was my imagination, but I felt he was responding a little to the excitement Tobé and I were showing. My usual reserve had disappeared, and I was banging my fists on the table and stamping my feet to the beat.

Before we knew it, it was after 3 AM, well past the legal closing time.

But not at Wally's. Shot glasses were put away, chipped tea cups were used for the strong stuff; the doors were locked, the lights lowered, and Louis was playing softly, through a mute, to the small audience remaining.

The Hi-Hat, Wally's and, later, George Wein's Storyville and Mahogany Hall gave me the opportunity to hear many jazz greats live: Sarah and Ella; The Count and The Duke; Brubeck and Shearing, among others. To hear (and meet) such musical innovators in the intimacy of those small clubs was a privilege that is no longer available.

Years later, I attended an outdoor amphitheater concert by Ella Fitzgerald, backed by the great Oscar Peterson Trio. They were famous by that time and played to an enthusiastic audience of more than a thousand. The hi-tech sound system was brilliant. Ella, my favorite scat singer, and Oscar were in top form. But it wasn't the same. Something was missing. Maybe it was those black sailors and the two white kids squeezed together in Wally's Paradise.

Through the years, jazz has been a place for me to go, a retreat from the world's meanness and madness and our workaday straitjackets. Sweet and sad, cool and sensual, jazz is a lesson and a gift, given freely by an oppressed people both to its own and to its oppressors.

I don't try to understand this music, but rather to be thankful for it and help to keep it a vibrant part of my life. It's just like the title of the final cut on my new jazz CDs, where Billie Holiday sings: "Don't Explain."

The Media's Odd Metamorphosis

Even though I hadn't worked full-time as a newspaperman (that's what I was called then) for more than three decades, the headlines still stung me. "Their mistakes were not honest; reckless, indefensible work poses a crisis for American journalism." "What's the scoop today? Profits, profits, profits. Journalism transformed for the worse." "Anchors are actors, not reporters."

And there was more. A star writer for *The New Republic* admitted he invented people and quotes in more than 20 highly praised magazine pieces. A talented poet hired as a columnist for the *Boston Globe* bit the dust after she admitted to the same grievous offenses.

CNN, the self-proclaimed 24-hour "news" network, was forced to retract a highly touted exclusive story they used to highlight the launching of a new operation. The story contended—without proof, it turned out—that the United States had used nerve gas against American defectors in Laos.

And what was the defense of award-winning war correspondent Peter Arnett, who anchored the "story"? He wasn't reporting, he said disingenuously, he was merely reading a script that was put in front of him. Arnett's defense is irresponsible and unconscionable. But, of course, CNN didn't fire him; it bounced some nameless producer instead.

Arnett, like me, is a graduate of the Associated Press school of news writing: Get it fast, but get it right. So what happened to him, and a lot of others like him?

It's easy to hypothesize that the evil temptress is television, with its huge paydays and the transformation of newspeople into designer-clad, well-coifed celebrities. And it's also easy to blame journalism's fall from grace on the merger craze that has swept the media into its greedy maw—much as had happened with telecommunications and professional sports.

With salaries vaulted into the millions, it is perhaps understandable that the Koppels, Rathers, Donaldsons and their now-wealthy colleagues have become too often fat and lazy talking heads who do little if any reporting. And with so much to protect, it is perhaps understandable that fact-checking takes a back seat to entertainment and titillation values.

Understandable, but not acceptable. Understandable, but disgusting in a free society that gave special protection to the press so it could serve as a voice for the powerless and shine the bright light of truth into the dark corners of corruption and lawlessness.

There is nothing wrong with newspeople, or sports stars for that matter, sharing in the huge profits they generate for the voracious corporations that own them. Television news, once barely a break-even operation offering viewers an essential service, has become a large profit center for the networks. Even the less glamorous newspaper writers are beginning to be paid decent wages, in line with the responsibility their profession calls them to.

So I'm making no plea for a return to the "good old days" when I was a reporter. In my day and before, we were held in very low repute. We were portrayed in books and movies mostly as hard-drinking cynics who would do just about anything to get a story (not that this was entirely untrue).

An anecdote that made the rounds then was of the less-than-proud mother whose first-born son was a reporter. When she was asked what he did for a living, she tried to make the picture a little brighter by responding: "He plays piano in a brothel." Thus, I was mystified when the family of my then-fiancée welcomed me with much respect. It turned out she told them I was a "journalist," a profession held in high esteem in Europe, from which they had recently emigrated.

Payscales were in keeping with our reputation. After nearly 15 years as an AP writer, and at the top of the scale of the American Newspaper Guild, I earned the princely sum of $9,412 a year. And with the exception of a few editors and couple of political columnists, I was about the highest paid reporter in my state of New Hampshire.

Out of a sense of fairness and balance, I have been ruminating about shoddy or dishonest reporting from my times. What comes most to memory are examples of misuse of the power of the press to gain personal or political agendas, and the beginnings of TV talk shows as the hothouse of sex and scandal.

On a national level, there was no more respected or powerful voice than columnist Walter Lippmann. While I can recall no instance of Lippmann manufacturing stories, there was little doubt he used his considerable weight to influence the direction of both domestic and foreign policy at the highest levels in Washington. And, more than once, he succeeded. Too often his words were not meant to inform his millions of readers so much as they were aimed to influence a few power-brokers.

Edward R. Morrow, who fairly can be said to have invented TV newscasting, and whose somber radio broadcasts from London as it was bombed during the early days of World War II helped to move America into the fray, had another side. He presided over a weekly TV talk show where he took us remotely into the homes of celebrities from Jack and Jackie Kennedy to Marilyn Monroe, and where he wasn't above squeezing out the gossipy details of their private lives.

Further down the food chain were the likes of Walter Winchell and Drew Pearson. Winchell, a one-time vaudeville performer, built enormous power through a tabloid gossip column in New York. His power became magnified with a radio, and later television, show where he mixed Broadway and Hollywood gossip with the bashing of President Roosevelt and the deification of J. Edgar Hoover and Sen. Joseph McCarthy.

Pearson's power came from knowing where all the bodies were buried and in which closets the skeletons were hidden in Washington. His column, "The Washington Merry Go Round," could make and break the powerful, often by innuendo alone.

I had a personal taste of Pearson's hubris and lack of fact-checking when I was a political operative and press secretary in Washington during the '60s. Pearson called my boss to check on some pretty shoddy stories making the rounds about a home state Congressman from the other side of the political fence. I was assigned the task of checking things out as best I could, and putting together information for Pearson.

Out of habit, I wrote my information in the form of a news story and included a cover note pointing out the need to verify and check further. Weeks later, my story appeared just about word-for-word as part of a Pearson column, never having been checked.

In the state of New Hampshire, charges of unfairness, bigotry and just plain lying were often hurled in the direction of William Loeb and his papers—the *Manchester Union Leader* and the *New Hampshire Sunday News*. In my memory, there was little proof of prevarication but a lot of fodder for charges of racism, political chicanery and malicious and outrageous ranting on the editorial pages.

Whatever the criticism, Loeb and his minions used the power of the press to end a long tradition of moderation (with flashes of liberalism) in the state's ruling Republican Party. They helped launch a new era of ultra-right activism.

As for my own reporting days, the rule—especially on a wire service like the AP—was "Just tell the news, please." Opinions, random thoughts and "what ifs" had no place in a news story. And the people we reported on knew it.

One evening the phone rang at our home, and Dina told me, "The governor is calling." In my bylined story of his news conference that morning, I wrote that Gov. Wesley Powell had on one issue become "red in the face, and pounded on his desk." Pretty tame stuff by today's standards.

But Powell, a one-time circuit-riding preacher who was sometimes given to oratorical excess, was furious. What right did I have to characterize his emotions in the news story? My defense that I was merely reporting the truth cut no ice with him, and our relations were strained for some time.

Did I ever make up a quote or invent an unnamed source? No. Did I ever "clean up a quote" so that it made more sense and parsed grammatically? Occasionally. Did I ever put my byline on someone else's work? No, but some of my work once appeared under the byline of a Pulitzer Prize winning journalist.

Our two-person AP bureau in Concord normally handled all the news in the state. But on special occasions, such as a vacation visit by President Eisenhower and our famous first-in-the-nation presidential primary, the AP would send in its first team.

About a week before a key primary (it was rumored Eisenhower was considering dumping Richard Nixon as his second-term running mate), one of the AP's giants arrived at our little closet of an office in the old Concord Monitor building. About the first words out of his mouth were "Where the hell is the Jack Daniels?" The AP had a tough rule about no booze in the office. But I wasn't about to argue, and hit the snowy streets to the state liquor store.

After satisfying his considerable thirst, he told us he was going to write a four-part series on the primary and the Nixon situation. He sat down at my old Remington standard and typed his name and a lead sentence on each of four sheets of copy paper. Then he said to me and my colleague, "You guys fill in the rest; you know all the local stuff. I've got to do some field work."

After he left, my partner and I shared some choice words about this guy's gall, then wrote the four stories and put them on the wire. Our anger—or perhaps jealousy—was fueled further because we knew just what his "field work" was. He carried on a quadrennial affair with an attractive woman connected with a daily newspaper. We didn't see him again until the evening of the primary. Ah, the divine right of kings.

As for sex and the media, just about the steamiest we experienced was when New Hampshire's Grace Metalious caused a sensation in New York literary circles with the publication of her *Peyton Place*. We were ordered to head up her way, find her and get an interview. Well, the interview itself proved rather boring. More interesting was trying to locate the author—finding her in company in a barn off the beaten track.

The bottom line is that the excesses of my day, some of which certainly were egregious, pale beside the profit-driven cynicism and outright dishonesty that characterize too much of today's media.

In my day we were skeptical, if not cynical, of the institutions of power, both public and private. Today it is all too acceptable for an institution like David Brinkley to become a paid honcho for a giant conglomerate.

In my day we wouldn't be caught dead socializing with the people we reported on, even if they wanted to have anything to do with us—which was unlikely. Today we don't blink when a syndicated columnist like George Will helps President Reagan prepare for campaign debates, or when White House reporter Britt Hume plays tennis on a regular basis with President Bush, the first.

We did not get paid for appearing on televised press conferences. Today, journalists get rich on political talk shows, sharing intelligence their primary employers (and we consumers) have already paid them for.

So was everything better in the old days? Absolutely not. By and large, today's young reporters are more highly educated, well informed and better writers than we were in our early days. Also, there is no honor in being underpaid and under-valued. And despite the worrisome loss of competition through merger-itis, many of today's smaller community newspapers are far superior to those of 30 or 40 years ago.

But none of the improvements mitigates the fact that it is wrong to make up stories or quotes or sources. It is wrong to quote from supermarket tabloids without fact checking. It is wrong to lift raw garbage from the internet or to lionize gossipmongers like Matt Drudge. It is wrong for Peter Arnett to cash in on the trust of his millions of viewers by acting as an ignorant reader—and then using his ignorance as a defense.

It is wrong for the most exalted and "serious" voices in American journalism to be reporting and analyzing pompously about a supposed semen stain on a young woman's dress, while finding little to say about 40 million Americans with no health insurance, 20 percent of our kids hungry and living in poverty, the intrinsic sinfulness of welfare "reform," or the class warfare that boosts the Dow Jones Average to astronomical heights while making the middle class the victims of merger-madness.

On a chill December day some 210 years ago, the first 10 additions of the Constitution were adopted. The first of these included the words: "Congress shall make no law . . . abridging the freedom of speech, or of the press . . ."

Those in the media, and their masters in conglomerate America, who see these words only as giving license and protection are missing an equally important part of their meaning: that with these rights comes responsibility, individual responsibility. In a free society, to quote President Kennedy, "our privileges can be no greater than our obligations. Each can be neglected only at the peril of the other."

Wandering in a Land of Poverty and Voodoo

I t was the empty look on the faces of the spindly-legged kids, pressed on us day after day in newspaper and television images, that brought old memories to the surface with a razor-sharp quality.

In April 1952, as a young Naval reservist, I ventured outside the United States for the first time, courtesy of the government. Destination: Haiti.

This mission was to give part-time sailors like me experience at sea, against the time when we might be called up to active service in the Korean conflict. The destination had no significance. Quite the opposite. Haiti was a place where servicemen could raise hell, a playground for Americans in uniform where no one cared about the impact on local people.

As I made my way up the gangplank of a decrepit World War I-era destroyer escort, I felt a mixture of fear and excitement. Ahead lay a 4,000-mile roundtrip on the open sea, on an outdated ship only as long as a football field, manned in large part by weekend sailors as ignorant of seamanship as I was. I had never before ventured farther to sea than the swan boats in the Public Garden in Boston. Yet, I was excited by the challenge to visit a place of mystery, the island home of voodoo.

The voyage south was, by turn, boring and terrifying. From the time we left Boston, there was little to see but the slate gray ocean and our companion ship, sailing about a mile off our port side. I was proud my stomach seemed seaworthy enough to keep down the Navy chow, including treats baked by a weekend seaman who was a pastry chef at a fancy hotel.

The calm came to an end when we slipped into the dangerous waters off Cape Hatteras, NC. A full-scale gale was raging, and it was my duty, as helmsman in training, to steer the ship from midnight to 4 AM. The full-time sailor assigned to train me had nothing but contempt for reservists. He delighted in blowing cigarette smoke in my face, which already had taken on a sick shade of green. The officer of the deck, waves washing over him on the bridge, shouted to me, over and over, "On you helm!" Translation: I was steering off course and toward our sister ship.

Miraculously, I avoided a collision. When my watch was over, I made my way below decks and strapped myself into my sack to avoid being pitched onto the steel deck in my sleep.

By morning, everything had changed. We were cruising off the south Florida coast. The sun was shining and the water was bluer than the sky. Dolphins leaped at ship-side. Every off-duty sailor, including me, stripped to skivvies and lay on the afterdeck, soaking in the warmth as the ship glided into the waters of the Caribbean.

The two ships anchored off Port-au-Prince in a torrid heat punctuated by brief downpours. We lined up for inspection, nervously hoping the creases would stay in our starched white uniforms long enough for us to make it ashore for the weekend. Given the okay, we crowded aboard the liberty boats, which moved ashore and tied up at the docks where we got our first close look at Haiti.

At dockside, there were rows of stalls with everything for sale that could be woven or carved by hand. I bought for my mother, after an hour of bargaining, a mahogany salad set for a dollar.

It was not until a few shipmates and I decided to walk into town that the reality of Haiti sank in. The pictures of Port-au-Prince then were little different from the picture now. Trees and greenery flourished in the hillsides where the Haitian overlords and British and American expatriates lived in comfort and safety, but there was no vegetation in the low-lying ghetto. There were only miserable huts, with no windows or doors, open to the hordes of flying pests that multiplied in the infested creeks that served as a sewage system and ran along the rows of shacks.

When the American navy was in town, most of the adults were busy adding to their income which, at that time, averaged about $100 a year. But it was the children, the small children, who remain in memory. We saw them sitting alongside those awful canals, staring blankly, not even bothering to sweep the flies away from their faces.

In the slums of Haiti only seven out of every 10 kids live longer than two years. The seven "lucky" ones can look forward to a life of perpetual hunger, disease and degradation.

The numbers tell an awful story. Haiti is a country of 7 million where almost 100 of every 1,000 babies die at birth, compared with nine here. People who get past childhood can expect to live only 55 years, 22 years less than you and me.

In the 45-plus years since my visit, the average family income has risen only to $250. Only 24 percent of the people in Haiti have any kind of sanitary services. Six in 10 have unsafe drinking water. And 4.5 million cannot read.

But the most awful thing is that in the intervening years since, as a young sailor, I spent three days on that God-forsaken island, not a single thing has happened to change the mean lives of these innocent people, except possibly to make them worse. The pictures that flash across our television screens are shocking to me only in that they duplicate what I saw in person nearly half a century ago.

I had been born into the Great Depression and brought up in working-class neighborhoods. But even the plight of the worst of the poor I lived among did nothing to prepare me for the sights and sounds I experienced that day. The cries of the hungry babies were thin and reedy, pitifully weak. The words of the teenage boy procuring for his stick-thin little sister I remember, word for word, all these years later: "You wanna buy my sister, Joe? She only 13, a virgin, Joe. You wanna buy her, just two dollar?"

We came to Haiti at Easter time. Much of the valley population was Catholic, and Easter—even, or especially, for the poor—was a time of celebration and pageantry.

On Sunday morning, the entire army and police force were at attention in the huge square fronting the cathedral. Through an opening in their ranks came the church fathers, their long surplices adorned with splashes of brilliant color.

Thousands of Haitians crowded around the periphery in a giant arc, singing songs of praise in a French graced by island idioms. Many danced, while some fell to their knees as the princes of their church passed by. My buddies and I were awestruck by this display, but when it was over we had something quite different planned.

The night before, as we drank rum and Coke in a joint called the Royal Cabaret, we asked the bartender where we could see voodoo. At first he did not answer but, encouraged by a few American dollars, he wrote something on the back of a printed card for the bar. It said: "Johnny Handrich. Taxi: No. 3271."

We found Mr. Handrich. After some persuasion and a promise of a tip to match the fare, he said he would drive us to a mountain site but would stop a mile short of the place and wait for us. The ride up the one-lane dirt road to the mountaintop can modestly be described as death defying. Johnny kept turning his head to talk to us while he barely negotiated the curves.

Suddenly he stopped and announced he would go no farther. He told us there were voodoo rites concurrent with Easter season and directed us to a stand of trees in the distance. With the mix of courage and carelessness often found in the young, we followed Johnny's directions and hid among the trees.

The voodoo ceremonies were under way. A couple of dozen people, mostly women and young men, were gathered in a clearing. The women wore turbans and sarong-like garments, all in a dazzling mixture of colors. Some of the young men were playing instruments, tapping out rhythms for the others, who were dancing flat-footed and holding strange objects.

One woman swung a live chicken above her head while reciting an incantation. But before the chicken could meet its fate, we were discovered. We turned to run back to the safety of Johnny's cab, but we were invited, in English, to join the group. Curiosity overcame fear, and soon we were sitting in a circle on the ground in conversation with those folks.

Suddenly there appeared, as if from nowhere, a supply of souvenirs for the Yankee sailors. I bought two voodoo dolls, and my buddies did likewise.

As we crowded back into the taxi and Johnny began his wild descent, it crossed my mind that we had been given front-row seats at a performance for the benefit of American sailors with dollars. In retrospect, I believe the experience was real, but that we were in a society so poor that even an important religious ritual must be interrupted for dollars to feed the kids.

Johnny dropped us at dockside as the sun was setting and shore liberty was coming to an end. Some of our less sober shipmates were being returned stretched out in rows in a shore patrol truck. A chief petty officer, who had located a motorcycle and way too much rum, whipped right by us and drove the bike off the end of the dock. He survived; the Harley didn't.

Determined to return without a penny, I gave my last dollar to a dock peddler for two monkeywood candy dishes. A tropical moon shone a silver path across the sea as we weighed anchor and began the long journey home.

Flying Old Glory with Pride

We had an old-fashioned Fourth of July last Sunday. And I relearned an old lesson about democracy. In the morning, Dina and I strolled through White Park. Clusters of kids were splashing in the pool, while others were climbing, sliding and swinging in the new, community-built Monkey-Around Playground. Parents were picnicking and stretching in the sun. Radios were playing, and there was a lot of laughter.

On this July 4, everything was great! We had been invited to an old-fashioned block party by our friends, Donna and Steve. With city approval, they had closed off both ends of the street. When we arrived, neighborhood kids were dashing in and out of a sprinkler in the middle of the street, screaming with delight as they soaked each other (and me) with water-filled balloons.

Paul Revere and the Raiders blared from a radio as we sat in the mid-day sun and sipped cool lemonade. The children's artwork was displayed—American flags, rockets, fireworks, and a hand lettered sign saying "Happy Birthday America."

Back at our home, an American flag was flying above our front steps. I had purchased the banner—one of those with the independence year "76" encircled by 13 stars—from an old flag store the previous winter. It was the first time in the 45 years since I left my parents' home that I had either owned or flown the flag.

When I was a kid, patriotism and the flag were not self-conscious things. Whether or not burning the flag was constitutional never came up, since no one considered that as a solution to anything. And patriotism was as indivisible as the "one nation" saluted in the pledge of allegiance.

My father, one of the youngest World War I veterans (he had signed up before his 14th birthday), had a miniature uniform made for me, and I marched proudly at his side in the Memorial Day and Fourth of July parades down Main Street in our home town.

Even though we were damn near poor, Dad always found a few

bucks to buy a box full of fireworks. At dusk, all the neighbors would congregate in our back yard, and when it got dark, the Roman candles and fountains would shoot up rainbows of color. The two-inch salutes sounded like cannons when they exploded in the empty trash barrels, into which we dropped them.

There wasn't a person there whose family had been in the United States for more than one generation. So, despite the fact that there was much wrong about America in the mid 1930s, despite the fact that no one in that yard had much money, those good people appreciated that they were better off than their immigrant parents, and realized that America was still an experiment in the making—with the future in their hands.

I grew up taught that there were hateful things going on around us, but that in no other nation would they be curable, and that we, the people, were responsible for coming up with the cures.

Somewhere along the line, that feeling got lost. It became fashionable to complain about what was wrong with America—not to do anything about it, mind you—and rather unsophisticated to brag about what was admirable.

Self-absorption largely has replaced compassion. People begging food for their families, we are told, must not be "spoiled" with handouts. Let them pull themselves up by their bootstraps, preach those who already have theirs, never looking to see the others have no boots. One of every four kids in America doesn't get enough to eat? Blame those damn Welfare Queens that our leaders so courageously unmasked for us.

The savings and loan crooks, who cost us honest saps half a trillion bucks, have paid back only about a penny on the dollar of court-assessed fines? Leave those boys alone. After all, didn't someone once say that the business of America is business?

I reject as un-American greed and egocentrism, disdain and ignorance, racism, bigotry and separatism, the rich getting richer and the poor living on the streets. And I reject the idea that the impulses of superiority and meanness that feed these evils have anything whatsoever to do with "family values."

I learned my American values from Norman Thomas, the Socialist; Abe Lincoln, the Republican; from Hubert Humphrey, the Democrat;

from Barry Goldwater, the conservative; Mario Cuomo, the liberal; Nelson Rockefeller, the moderate. From Martin Luther King, the black minister; Muhammad Ali, the Muslim; Harry Truman, the Protestant; Cesar Chavez, the Catholic; Isaac Bashevis Singer, the Jew.

My family values I learned from my immigrant Orthodox Jewish grandparents, and my other grandparents, Dutch Socialists; and from what was left of my wife's family of Holocaust survivors. And from my father who always worked like a dog, and my mother, who suppressed her talents and any bitterness, so they could bring up my brother and me the best they could; and from my friends and associates, and— proudly—from my wife and our children, who reflect decent values, both family and American.

So, I'm taking out a new option on my patriotism, and restoring my hope for the America yet to come. I'm flying the flag again, not only for what this nation has given me and mine, but also in recognition of the unfinished work ahead for us all if the dream shared by Jefferson, Lincoln, and Martin Luther King ever is to become reality.

Last Sunday, as darkness set the backdrop for soaring fireworks displays at Memorial Field, and as the 218th Independence Day drew to a close, I was reminded of American folk hero Woody Guthrie's seminal song about our nation's basic values of inclusion, equality and sharing of bounty:

> This land is your land, this land is my land,
> From California to the New York island;
> From the redwood forests, to the
> Gulf Stream waters,
> This land was made for you and me.
> This land was made for you and me.

The Joy and Pain of Life

I Choose Madness

"A man needs a little madness, otherwise
he will never cut the rope and be free."
Zorba the Greek

I know now that always I have been a little mad, but have never considered using it to get free. My madness is at least partly genetic, some weakness in the family strain, mostly on my father's side. His father was a particularly dull-witted man, and two of his uncles were marginally retarded. His brother was what once was called "not bright." And my only sibling lived for thirty years in a state institution.

My mother's mother was a depressive; there was one aunt who was in and out of mental institutions, and my mother herself had a "nervous breakdown" after a miscarriage.

Adding to the broth, there were streaks of brilliance in both families. One uncle was a legal scholar, Rhode Island's first Jewish attorney general, and on the way to the governorship when he was stricken with Lou Gerhig's disease. My mother's father, a voracious reader and spellbinding orator, was an early leader in the labor movement. My father's grandfather, Naphtali (after whom I'm named), was a renowned poet and cantor. The mythology, if not the science, of disturbed and/or dull broods always includes the occasional shooting star.

All my life, it's clear now, I have been a few points off true North on the compass called Normality. At times I have used my madness to some advantage, and at others it has overwhelmed me.

Until recently, I was a mass of anxieties and black fears. For three decades I could not fly in planes. Hyperventilation brought on terrifying symptoms of heart attack and brain tumor. These coalesced into a several-year-long clinical depression that rendered me as helpless as a beached whale.

Whether this off-centeredness has contributed to my creative abilities and energies, is still in question. I would like to believe there is a positive Yang to my strange Yin. For example, I am a hopeless romantic on the inside, goal-oriented obsessive—with a touch of the martinet—on the outside. A control freak by day, a poet and painter by night. A rager against injustice, a mistake-maker of epic proportion. A believer in community, yet never quite an inside part of one. A lover of quiet in the night, yet at times an impatient, hollering bully. A lover of people, but with no bosom friends and feeling increasingly lonely and alienated. A man much closer to death than birth with no closure in sight. One who at times despairs of life and its meaning, yet finds no sense in intentionally ending it.

The ocean brings me some relief and definition. Because it is so huge and immutable, it makes me feel insignificant enough so that my wackiness and woes just don't matter much. There I pray to the water, and talk and sing to the rocks, especially the ebony ones. I croon lines from romantic tunes as mantras to the sun as, at sunrise, it peeks over the horizon. I walk the near empty autumn beach, hoping to meet magical people—and sometimes I do.

I believe in magic now—and auras and voiceless communication, transcendence and maybe even pre- and re-incarnation. Maybe!

I yearn to do correctly now all the stuff that before I did wrong, or was afraid to do, or didn't trust myself enough to do. I want young women in summer dresses to have crushes on me. I want to read them the poems I wrote 50 years ago, when I should have read them on first dates. I want to croon love songs and sad songs to doe-eyed girls in bobby socks and penny loafers. I want to have dreams and ambitions, and to experience self-worth and self-consciousness, as I didn't then.

I want to go back in time to drive my father's big, black Packard town car—which he never allowed me to do. I want my mother—a fantastic dancer in her era—to teach me to ballroom dance, which she never did.

I want to walk again down to Malden Square with my great grandpa, Isaac Peekel, him holding my hand, me feeling safe and taken care of. I can't remember that feeling—being taken care of.

I want to go back to high school and get all As, which I could have done, instead of failing course after course, in a cry—never heard—for attention. I want to join the debating team and write for the school newspaper and yearbook, and try for a college scholarship; I would have been successful at them all.

I want to develop the real me instead of donning costumes for pleasing others and adapting to their needs. I want to be a leader; I want to be popular and sought after.

I want Zorba's kind of madness—to dance a Greek dance beside the Aegean, and sing songs of love and death; to eat ocean creatures and drink young wine from a leather flask; to laugh from the stomach and make love with a strange young woman just because it feels good and has the odor of life; to tear off my shirt and dive deep into the sea . . . . .

I see brother death just around the corner. Like Zorba, I spit in his eye, and choose madness over fear.

My Acre of Land on the Moon

n 1953, when I bought an acre of land on the moon for one dollar, I came in for a lot of ribbing. But these days, with moon landings in the realm of the ordinary, I'm standing tall.

My vindication came 45 years after my lunar purchase, which was viewed by all then as the act of that related word—lunatic.

Robert Bigelow, a real estate and hotel tycoon from Las Vegas, announced he will build a 100-passenger luxury rocket-ship that will cruise up to and around the moon. Also, he's pledged to invest half a billion dollars in a new space tourism company.

I am taking this realization of my vision with all the modesty I can muster. But I can't help noticing the changes in attitude all around me. For example, my wife no longer turns deep scarlet and pretends to faint when I offer to show dinner guests my "interplanetary moon kit, including a quit-claim deed to one acre on the moon and a map showing its location."

And people have become moon-minded. They don't even express doubt as to my mental balance—at least not out loud—when I tell them how someday there will be a little vacation cottage called "My Blue Heaven" on a quiet lunar lagoon.

Before the moon-kit arrived, I got my adventure second-hand from books, television and the movies. Only in my reveries did I rescue fair damsels in distress, swim channels and score touchdowns before screaming crowds of thousands.

Then one day I spotted a newspaper editorial, in the *Wall Street Journal* of all places. It was headed: "Moon Land for Sale." Here was my chance to become an adventurer! The article said a former astronomer turned entrepreneur was issuing quit-claim deeds to one-acre tracts on the moon.

I didn't know what a quit-claim deed was (and I still don't), but my application and dollar bill were in the next mail. Then came two weeks of anxious waiting, sprinkled with doses of crude sarcasm from family and friends.

Finally, the moon kit arrived in an official-looking envelope bearing the fancy stamp of "Interplanetary Development Corp." Inside was a gilt-edged "General quit-claim deed to one acre of land on the Moon, northeast quadrant," assuring the party of the first part (that was me) to "that certain plot—Title No. A06437—piece or parcel of land lying and being in the crater Copernicus, situated in the northeast quadrant of the surface of the moon, facing the planet Earth."

But that wasn't all. I was to fall heir to "all mineral and oil rights, if any," free access to a beach and "right of access to the Sea of Tranquility for the enjoyment thereof." Also the right to fish and dig clams "upon and under the Sea of Nectar" was within my reach.

"Congratulations, neighbor," said the cover letter, "welcome to your moon." And there was a picture of two men in space suits, shaking hands. I guessed the one with the green head was a rep from the Lunar Chamber of Commerce. Then I took a look at the moon map, replete with gold mountains and blue craters, all neatly indexed by number and letter. Oh, oh. My acre seemed to be smack in the middle of a canal!

Undaunted, I turned to the last item in the kit, a post card assuring me of lifetime membership in the "Lunar Civic Association," and asking if I would like to reserve one seat on "our first passenger rocket to the moon." I signed up for the civic association, and heart a-beat, I also signed up for the rocket trip.

Said my best friend: "You're nuts."

That may be, and I may never get to the moon. But I'm not giving up hope. As the president of the Interplanetary Development Corp. wrote:

"Whatever you do, hang on to your deed to the Moon. You can never tell what exciting possibilities it may bring your way in the world of the day after tomorrow."

Feeling a Little Crazy?
Relax, It's Not Just You

Think you may be going bonkers? Are you angry and confused? Feel you may have spring fever? Well don't worry, it's not in your head. Here, from just one edition of the daily newspaper is part of what's going on in your world and mine:

The Big Boys in Washington and the military are out to destroy a top-flight female officer, principally for having an affair. Realizing what jerks they look like, they are now blubbering that she was someone entrusted with nuclear weapons who lied about her sex life. When the guys do it, it is "boys will be boys." When a woman does, it's a threat to national security.

What else happens when you give females too much freedom? Read this: "A study suggests that half of all chimpanzees may be conceived on the sly when females sneak off for risky trysts with males outside their social group." What do you expect when the males inside the group spend all day beating their chests and never take their women for romantic walks in the forest?

Government and politics keep making as much sense as usual. We continue to give China special trade favors, even though there is clear evidence of its repressive regime. Latest news is that U.S. companies apparently are selling illegally imported products made in prisons.

The administration wants to do away with restrictions, in place since the Great Depression, that keep banks, insurance companies and brokerages from going into each other's business. You don't suppose any bank would pressure you into using their insurance when they give you a house or car loan? Nah.

And to hell with dolphins. By nearly a hundred-vote margin, the House voted to lift the tuna import embargo, despite warnings that thousands of dolphins will be killed by certain tuna nets. Hey, business is business.

Our valiant president applauds while the Senate kills an effort to provide health care for 5 million poor kids by raising the cigarette tax.

"It's a budget buster," says Republican leader Trent Lott. The president is not about to see "all that hard work (on the budget) go down the drain," says a spokesman. But, don't worry, we've got Prez Bubba standing tall in the world of virtual reality. He took a whack at the fashion industry for using skinny models who look like they could be using heroin when they appear in TV ads. The ads are "ugly," says Mr. Clinton, apparently more so than 5 million kids who lack proper medical care.

And here's a shock: a new study shows that welfare "reform" will hit poor communities worse than wealthy ones. Also, it seems that scads of people, many of them neophytes, are trying to scale Mt. Everest, and the more that get killed in the effort, the more who try. Dr. Kavorkian, phone home.

In the world of sports, the usually redoubtable commentator Marv Albert was indicted on charges of forcing sex on a woman and biting her 15 times. Now the woman is facing a charge she threatened to kill a cheating ex-boyfriend and his dog. Yessssss!

World chess champ Garry Kasparov is teed off. He says the computer who beat him was somehow fixed, thus making "the sporting contest unfair." He demands a million-dollar rematch. He says money has nothing to do with it. Right.

Wait, it gets nuttier. Down in Florida a 12-year-old girl has been moved from her catcher's position on a boys/girls Babe Ruth baseball team because she won't wear a jock strap and protective cup. The league commissioner, badly in need of an anatomy lesson, says it's for the girl's protection. "It's no different than her (face) mask."

One doctor says he would "not apply a boys device to a girl." The head of the local National Organization of Women, chimes in with wondering how boys would like it if they had to wear bras. The girl's mother gets to the heart of the matter: "She's not going to wear a boy's cup over a penis she doesn't have."

Over in Maryland, officials are shooting mute swans because, they say, there are too many of them. If mute swans are as quiet as their name implies, how about knocking off some of those noisy, and less beautiful, crows? Just kidding, Audubon Society.

In Vermont, a 72-year old man, (more than likely with the advice of his friendly attorney), is seeking $300,000 in damages from a bicycle rider who hit him from behind causing physical and emotional pain. The suit says the bicyclist "should have known that bicycles are to be ridden with care," and he was driving "in a careless manner." At the time of the incident, the kid riding the tricycle was six years old. Did anyone get his blood alcohol level?

"Just Because" Isn't Enough

"**J**ust because." That was the heart of the reason a woman gave for wanting to locate a child she gave up for adoption 37 years ago. She wanted, the newspaper article said, to answer that now-grown man's questions, to see if he is healthy and happy, and whether she has any grandchildren "who looked at the world through her eyes, felt breezes blow through her hair, charmed adults with her smile."

"Closure is certainly a big part of it," she added.

As the father of two adopted children—who came into our lives at about the same time the woman gave up her baby—I hardly know where to begin to respond to this rather cloying and one-sided story. First, though, I want to say I can empathize with the pain, longing and curiosity this woman professes. She is entitled to them.

What she may not be entitled to is the right to hurt and confuse other, innocent people, just because, as she is quoted: "He's my son, dammit, and I want to see the magic thing I created."

The "magic thing" she created, if my experience is any judge, was for the adoptive parents a tiny bundle of love and joy whose diaper seemed always in need of changing, whose colic kept him up screaming for months, whose bronchitis meant scary nights in a steam-filled bathroom. It meant feeding, housing and clothing him. It meant a helpless human being with needs to be filled.

For the prospective adoptive parents, it meant a "gestation" period of 12, not 9 months, before their parenthood became legal. It was a time of uncertainty and fear that the child they have come to love could be taken away at any time. It meant being under the watchful eye of the state's social workers, who could knock on the door any day, unannounced. It meant being under the jurisdiction of the probate court until the temporary and then final adoption decree came down.

It meant doctor's visits, emergency room stops for stitches, problems in school, driver's licenses, first dates, proms, college tuition, the pain of separating when the kids moved out, engagement parties, weddings, meeting new families of in-laws, almost losing a loved daughter-in-law at the birth of a first grandchild. And so much more of the joy and pain of life.

In short, the "magic thing" may have been created at birth, but that "thing" became a person through the environment in which he grew up. It is called nurturing. It means years of non-judgmental love. It includes teaching that small miracle how to walk, talk, learn, and to appreciate music and art and football. How to respect women, how to detest prejudice, how to share one's good fortune.

We live in a world that, increasingly, assures us that there are no consequences for our actions. Four decades ago, most women lived in a time when they had "no choice" but to give up their children; however, their pregnancies were in most cases a result of their own actions.

The article says a new law making it easier for birth parents and children to locate each other puts the decision "with the two people who were there when the relinquishment took place and were most affected by it . . . ." But there were other people "there" (perhaps in the background) at the time—two people who were themselves in pain at being childless; two people waiting to lavish love upon a child who had been conceived by strangers; two people who did not judge the birth parents; two people who pledged, legally as well as emotionally, their lives, their fortunes and their undying support to a tiny infant.

Those were the people gladly willing to accept the consequences and the responsibility. And, of course, receive the love that only results from parenthood. Let us pay some attention to their possible anguish, and maybe that of their child and grandchild, when a stranger comes knocking at their door, saying she needs "closure."

In the Depths of Depression

The passage of time filled me with guilt, so I kept myself from looking at a clock. But it was difficult to avoid the glaring green numbers on the VCR, reciting the march of time, minute by minute.

It was 1:30 on a typical afternoon and I was—as usual—still in my pajamas, lying on the sofa staring absent-mindedly at the obsequious Richard Dawson and Family Feud on TV. It was television with which I spent the most time for some three years; it blinked and talked at me from the time I woke with despair in late morning, until, finally, it put me into a fitful sleep usually about 2 AM.

My shame for spending nearly all of my waking hours prone in front of the television was exacerbated by my inability to do anything about it. And on those infrequent days when I forced myself to get up, shave and dress, that was about as far as I got. My small surge of energy would dissipate in a wave of anxiety.

I couldn't bring myself to go to the office of my already faltering business. I was deterred because I knew there would be mail to deal with and phone messages on the answering machine. I hadn't returned calls for many weeks; at home I never answered the phone. Mail piled up and was stuffed, unopened, into large manila envelopes, and stowed in the basement.

I seldom ventured downtown during those years for fear I would bump into someone I knew. The few times I couldn't avoid being on Main Street, I would avert my face or race across the street when a familiar person approached.

Operating the car was a major effort. Driving downtown at times caused a feeling of dizziness; locating a parking space was often more than I could handle, and I'd find myself back in my own garage. On trips I would drive only on main highways, armed with a small library of maps and detailed, typewritten directions. Once, on the way to visit friends, we got half way when I had a panic attack, turned around and went back home.

On the few occasions it was impossible to avoid going to a party or gathering of friends, I would be ravaged by paranoia. Among friends of 25 years, I felt alone, separated by an invisible wall from the laughter and camaraderie. When I ventured to speak a sentence or two, it seemed to me I was ignored by everyone. I was jealous of their easy conversation, and angry that they were getting on with their lives without me.

Voices drifted in and out like on a distant radio station. I wondered how I looked to them. Could they tell? Would they be on the phone the next day talking about me? Why the hell couldn't I laugh anymore?

I knitted together a life of lies, manufacturing elaborate excuses for my monastic existence and strange behavior. It became easier and easier to blame others for my own bizarre situation. Those closest to me were pulled slowly but surely into my faux world; it was their only way to communicate with me.

Physicians provided a variety of medications, one pill to perk me up, another to calm me down. They didn't work. For anyone who hasn't yet put a name to my affliction, during those black times I was sunk in a clinical depression.

Even now, I have no clear idea of just how I wandered into that sad and lonely state. Sure, I can isolate events at that time: illnesses, an unfriendly business partnership split, what seemed at age 54 like a hurtling toward the last stage of life, a feeling of having largely squandered my real talents. Maybe those things were plenty.

Or was it also in the family? I can remember my mother having what was called a "minor nervous breakdown" after a miscarriage. But that lasted only a short time.

Was it something in me, something building over many years? I was in some ways an alienated youngster, brought up in a neighborhood where your place in the pecking order was determined by how well you could fight and how well you played sports. I was not much good at either, and besides I was surreptitiously scribbling poems in the late night hours. A private person, I spent my early years crowded into a six-room flat with seven other family members from four generations. I had no privacy.

I believe it was an agglomeration of those things and others, telling a mind and body to shut down for a while, and then re-group.

The road back from that dark place was no less confusing than the path that took me there. I do know at some point my self-loathing and my desire to get back in the game coalesced around the idea that I needed some help, a guide. Given my background, I equated the concept of seeing a psychologist with personal weakness and self-absorption. But now I was desperate, fearing that soon there might be no way back.

I took a leaf from the book of my wife, who often quoted this proverb: "If you're going to fall from a horse, fall from a big horse." So not only did I make an appointment with a psychologist, but I chose a woman psychologist. Can you imagine?

In retrospect it is clear that the clash of egos and macho games I would have played with a male could have blocked any chance for recovery. It is also clear that this woman (who is now a valued friend) quickly got my number and exercised an unusual kind of patience.

For about a year, I told her almost nothing but half-truths and outright lies. "Are you cutting back on TV?" she would ask. Sure, I would reply, saying I was setting two daily hour-long TV blackouts. Lie. How about the daily walk? "Well, I'm getting started, about twice a week." Lie. "Are you reading the help-wanted ads," she wondered? "I'm beginning to circle a few jobs, and will call soon." Lie.

My sons tried to help in every way they could. I can imagine now how tough it must have been for them to see their dad in a condition that society has stamped embarrassing and unacceptable. Once, during a session, they both showed up at the psychologist's office, in an attempt at a strategy called intervention. It was supposed to shock me into reality; instead I was mortified, although I realized it took real love for them to make the effort. My older son dropped off the help wanted section every Sunday, and put together for me a loose-leaf book of "things to do today." I found it recently in the basement—not a word had been written on any page.

Things were no easier for my wife, who, among other things, had to trek home from work every noon to fix and eat lunch with me, something I would not do on my own. To say I was something less than a good mate during those times would be an understatement. On one occasion, when I agreed to accompany her and another couple to a concert, I took an extra pill to ensure I would remain calm, and promptly fell asleep on the shoulder of our friend, snoring out of time with the music. After that, we just didn't accept such invitations.

At the height of the therapy, I was going two or three times a week. This presented further problems. Should I park in front of the office and dash in quickly, but risk having someone recognize my car or license plate outside the building? Or should I park around the corner and take the chance someone would see me walking, and want to stop to chat? There seemed no end to these dilemmas which, in retrospect, seem so minor.

So it went, month after month, with no seeming improvement. Then the tide began to turn in two ways. First, I was feeling enormous guilt at lying to myself and this caring woman, even going so far as to rehearse the stories I would tell her before each session. Finally, I began to admit the truth of my situation. Also, I made the first call seeking employment, overcoming my awful fear of rejection.

Now that the con game was over, things began to change. I was able to hear what the therapist was asking and suggesting. Since she was a student of Eastern thought and meditation as well as "regular" practice, her prescriptions went beyond single-syllable responses and answering questions with questions. They included showing she cared, respect for the patient, some shared tears and imaging. And these things worked.

But not right away. I tried, with no success, to locate my "center," that spot in the belly from where peace and equanimity emanate. I read books about levels of consciousness and how the proper diet paves the road to mental health. No help. Deep breathing brought on hyperventilation. But I realize now that it was in the trying that I broke the cycle of depression.

However, the anxieties remained. It was a single image that seemed to work with them. My friend would end each session with these words or others like them: "There is a doorway. Beyond there is a fog or mist. To walk through your anxieties, just walk through that door. Walk through just once, and they will be gone."

Did I ever walk through that doorway? Well, perhaps not literally. But it was at that point that all my anxieties vanished. I believe the key was deciding I wanted to walk through the door. It was the decision that made the difference, rather than some walk in the fog, although I'm not prepared to discount that possibility entirely.

One morning shortly after that, I hopped out of bed at 7 AM, ate a big breakfast, and went to shower and shave. As I reached for my razor, my hand fell on my pill containers. I emptied all of them into the toilet bowl and, for the first time in quite a while, I smiled. The exact "how" my recovery came about remains largely a mystery.

Do I occasionally have days marked by feelings of depression or anxiety? Sure. But I use the tools I know I have to fight off the demons. And so far I've won the battles.

Will the course I took work for others? That I do not know. In my case, it yanked me back from a life of passivity and inertia into a time where I have been more creative and productive than ever before.

Fear Takes Flight

"**W**hen the speed gauge reaches 65, pull back gently on the stick." So said the young instructor sitting to my right in the small cabin of the single-engine Cessna 172. I took a deep breath, followed his instructions, and two wondrous things happened:

- The little airplane lifted gently off the runway at the Concord Airport and, with very little urging, climbed to 2,000 feet above the earth.

- For the first time in nearly 30 years, I was free of a mindless, but numbing fear that had assumed phobic proportions and limited my life. And, for the first time in 18 years, I was airbound.

My maiden flight was in the early '50s when, as a young wire service reporter, I traveled from Portland, Maine, to Logan Airport in Boston. I was not wild about the idea since a hurricane had just struck; but some of the roads were impassable, a very attractive young woman was waiting, and the Northeast Airlines DC-3 was my only option.

Later in the '50s when I was working in the Concord Associated Press bureau, Dina and I would often fly Northeast from Concord to New York, where we would indulge our passion for the theater. The flight would make a stop in Boston, which meant the plane would fly very low, making for stomach-churning bumps and sudden drops in altitude.

In the early '60s, we followed the Kennedy revolution to Washington, DC, where for the next six years I seemed to be as much in the air as I was on the ground. Not only did business flights take me all around the country, but also we took flying vacations to Nassau and Hawaii.

I never was wild about flying, but in those days some good conversation and a few libations generally would divert my nervousness and keep the sweaty-palm syndrome to a minimum. But a combination of running to catch flights, and the ennui of hours waiting for planes, along with what is popularly referred to as career "burnout," began to take their toll.

The climax was reached with a crashing (oops, poor choice of word) crescendo in one three-day trip with my boss, when we flew literally thousands of miles with seemingly endless takeoffs and landings. I can't put our schedule in order, but I remember we flew out of Washington National Airport on a Friday morning and stopped at Des Moines, Cleveland, Chicago, Austin, Dallas, and Fort Worth, among other places, and were back in DC, Sunday night.

What happened on that trip traumatized me for the next three decades. On the first leg, we had to get out of planes twice because of the ever-popular "mechanical problems." Then on the short flight from Fort Worth to Dallas on a turbo-prop plane, the pilot's windshield cracked, forcing a landing.

The trip was capped on the takeoff from Chicago headed back to Washington. The jet began its steep ascent as usual, but suddenly leveled off, and began to make chugging sounds. The No Smoking sign went on and we were instructed to fasten our seat belts. My boss, a licensed pilot himself, was in the window seat. As I turned to him to ask what happened, I saw that he had taken out his Rosary beads and was praying silently.

"What the hell's going on, Bernie?" I asked, knowing the answer was not going to be good. "One or two of our engines have flamed out," he said. I stretched and looked out the window; we were headed toward the city and some damn high buildings.

I felt a cold shiver, and moments later my face was bathed in sweat. I grabbed onto Bernie's arm and squeezed. Terror and hope fought for space.

"What's going to happen?"

"We're probably going down."

Obviously, we did not go down. Some combination—perhaps of prayer and pilot skill—intervened, and suddenly we felt a rush of power as the engines re-ignited, and that airplane shot nearly straight up like a missile. Saved! But not from the trauma of having to remain on that plane for the next three hours until we landed at National.

Between that day in 1966 and the day in 1998 when I took my first flying lesson, I had flown only twice. Once was a business trip from

Washington to Puerto Rico, when I broke the Guinness Book of Word Records' mark for number of martinis downed on a short flight over the Atlantic. The impetus for the flight: my job was on the line.

The other flight was in 1978, when we were invited by President Carter to attend the signing of the Israeli-Egyptian Peace Treaty. The import of the event mitigated my panic—but not by much.

How did I move from phobic fear to becoming, at age 65, a tyro enthusiast of airplanes? I'm not exactly sure. Part of it was when, a decade earlier, I made my way out of a clinical depression and began clearing away anxieties. Only the fear of flight remained, closing options, limiting choices, blocking growth.

I determined my fear was not of death (otherwise, what was I doing driving on the Maine turnpike on the Fourth of July weekend?), but seemingly a combination of claustrophobia and lack of control. After all, I had no fear of tall buildings, elevators, high bridges. Just this crippling fear of flying.

If there are such things as renewal and transcendence, I experienced them that sunny day as I gently urged the little plane to break the shackles of earth and head toward heaven.

At Sea

York, Maine, March 19—An oldies station is playing on the car radio . . . the eternal Don Ho singing "Tiny Bubbles," stirring memories of a long ago voyage to Hawaii: Warm breezes, sweet scents, beautiful people in all shades, placid blue water.

Before me this day the Nubble Lighthouse, a white starkness (rouged with red roofs) on an islet almost kissing shore, its Cyclopean eye casting a Laser-thin beam out from the coast of Maine. The ocean, a slate gray Don Ho never saw, beats against the Nubble's fringes, relentless, at high tide.

I sit alone in the week of my 65th birthday, away by myself. Watching the ocean, acutely aware of being and of being alone. The seacaps climb up and over the sides of the craggy land's end, pushing into the cracks and crannies, forming ponds in the hollows. My ego, crack'd like a bad-luck mirror those years ago, seems comfortably consumed, subsumed, by the force of the sea.

I take in a horizon that doesn't exist, yet draws the straightest of lines, broken only by toy-sized silhouettes of rusty freighters and asexual Love Boats. Alone finally. But alone at a beginning or an end? More likely another damned middle.

Alone, eyeing For Sale signs on small shingled cottages within sight or sound of the sea. For three decades I have been visiting and, in pain, leaving the Maine shore. Now, as the sand moves faster through my hour-glass, I feel the damn fool for never shifting the 60 short miles East.

How I yearn for a place at earth's edge, near my kind's original home. It comes to me: Alone is for unloading, accepting and planning for the last part. The last part . . . it will be a gentle time out there on the water. In that second I come to terms with death and I'm ready for a devil's pact with Ocean: Envelop me and set me free. You can have me when it's done. How much worse is a shark's belly than wormy earth? At once, I can talk to my eyes, listen to my skin, love my fingertips. At last I am within reach of sanity and reason, but I doubt that I will reach for them. The edge of madness has been my mate all these years, burning out the inertia of my soul.

Walking the smelly, low-tide flats, I collect stones and shells—only those dry of life, of course—to give to little Sarah. I'll tell her they have been waiting these eons just for her. We both will believe it. I carry little stones always in the pocket of my blue corduroy jacket, white, smooth stones. I dreamt once that I swallowed them all, putting to sleep forever my longing for flight, desire for lightness and escape from this gravitied graveyard.

Awareness of the difference between giving up and giving in. And, finally, giving in; sweet tears flow, no salt along my cheeks. Nothing to prove. A grain of sand slides down my throat, a seed from the crusty earth, caressed smooth by the water.

The gulls, white-winged garbage collectors of the shore, sit atop the quarter-fed telescopes that bring far water as close as near water. The sun squeezes between white striations, burning new holes into the cloudy cataracts stealing sight from my well-used eyes.

"Take our picture," says a waif-like girl in a white hat, politely but no question mark at the end. As I grasp her flat camera, her companion, a bent old man, inches his way out of an ancient Mercury, pushing himself erect with an aluminum cane. A black, leather glove masks his useless left hand. He smiles wanly through familiar pain. The girl's a Cheshire cat. Snap. Thanks. They're gone.

Two young women, shapely in tight tee shirts, scramble across the rocks. A crowd of gulls screeches around a man in a dark green loden coat as they snatch orange Cheez Doodles from between his fingers. He speaks in measured tones to the birds, now in a frenzy for the chemical crap he feeds them.

The sun has won its battle, and I stretch before it on a wooden bench. Gulls skim inches above my old, Greek fisherman's cap, but I am protected by the ragged remains of a yellow feather, stuck in the hat, found years earlier on an ocean island. The water's now a blue to suit even a Hawaiian. If it were warmer, I tell myself, I would strip off my clothes and take my ugly body down into the ocean.

A couple feeds Wonder Bread to the birds. "This one's salivating," the blond boy giggles to the blonde girl. A gull settles on the hood of my car, inches from my face, glass between us. Mindlessly, I begin a conversation. The bird shits, and flies away to join his kind.

> But he'll return to clean the dross
> That waters always push across
> Rubbish tossed thoughtlessly
> To make its way across the sea
> Now swallowed in a breadless lull
> By one unknowing white seagull.

York Beach, Maine, March 20—A different day, gray and foreboding, all noise—thunderous bursts of surf pounding on rock. Gulls different, too. More businesslike, flying, improbably, into a near-gale blow, looking like mimes pushing against non existent walls. Spent waves back away, leaving a new meal for the birds in the cracks and crevices. Bilious scum rides atop the waves, mixing with white foam into an ochre spume that spends itself against the rocks, spraying my face.

An ocean furious beyond its own control. A huge log tossed like a boomerang, back and forth between the eddies and undertow. Nattering rocks cobbling their way over sister rocks, toward sea . . . only to be pushed back by the next onrushing torrent. Drawn again to the Nubble; its Saab-sounding horn and laser-red ray hurl warnings made impotent by an impenetrable fog wall.

Mesmerized by this darkening cacophony, I walk close to the edge of the peninsula. A monster wave hits below, climbs the rock wall in an instant, crashes into me. I nearly topple over the precipice, but struggle back, a sopping clown, safe. Salt all in my eyes and ears, my mouth full, pebbles in my shoes. My clothes are plastered to my body, the cleansing salt eating into the raw edges of two cuts on my leg.

People stare but—amazingly—instead of being embarrassed I laugh. Taking this sweet victory as mine, I lick the salt from my beard, get in the car, and leave—the Nubble disappearing in the rearview window.

At Long Sands Road, the sea has found a weakness, and tosses a truckload of driftwood, seaweed and rocks across the boulevard.

A block down, the ocean pushes its way into the front yard of a crumbling house, eerie even in daylight. A quiescent salt pond has formed beside the peeling walls and broken porches, cracked windows, and aching roof. A wooden sign atop a tottering post in front, proclaims the house a "Tabernacle."

As I move past the ocean view, I spot a row of waves—thin, white soldiers falling, exhausted on the sand, their thousands-mile march ended.

> There are, in the end, no ways to tell about the sea—
> Not by daubing a canvas or by snapping a second
>   in time,
> or by filling a paper with words.
> For the sea itself is the Narrator, and talks only in
>   riddles.
>
> She is older than Man, older than the idea of Man,
>   older than God or any god.
> The sea is beyond bribery or bias, selecting sur-
>   vivors and victims at will and whim.
> Only the sea is mighty enough to fill the sky.
>
> It is not only the time of my birthday, but also the
>   Earth's
> It is the first day of Spring.
> The sea and I both are alive.
> We celebrate. Together.

ACKNOWLEDGEMENTS

Dina, whose husband I was for more than 47 years, did not live to see this book in print. But her quiet guidance, support without end, and belief in my ability to get it done are everywhere living in these pages.

For being our supportive and loving family, I owe much to our sons, David and Michael, our daughters-in-law, Meg and Lori, our grand-daughter, Sarah, and my brother, Stephen.

For my painful, but important, education on the Holocaust, I am indebted to Dina and her family, notably her oldest surviving brother, Al, one of the important narrators from that time of black horror.

Deep gratitude also to the men and women of blessed memory whose spirits live with me still. Great Grandpa Isaac; Grandparents Sarah and Aaron, and Frank and Rose; our darling daughter, Laurie Beth, whose light shone for a brief nine months; and of course, the rest of the mishpocheh.

Not forgotten either are the friends of my youth—Charlie, Stanley, Donnie, Lennie, Dickie, and the swell girls who occasionally took pity on me. Thank you, too, to Sen. Tom McIntyre and Bernie Boutin, my bosses in the Washington years, who gave me opportunity, support and an education.

Whatever credit and kudos are due this volume must be shared with a support system including Roy Morrison, for his editing, shaping, cheerleading and patience; Maggie van Galen, editor, transcriber, good friend; my associates in Writers Publishing Cooperative; my students at the Brandeis University Adult Learning Institute for teaching me as they learned.

In other words, I have been blessed since the beginning by the wonderful people who have trod the path with me, helping me over the bumps, giving of their energy and strength.

A number of these pieces appeared first in my hometown newspaper, the *Concord Monitor.* I thank the *Monitor* and its editor, Mike Pride, for opening its pages to me over the years, in the great tradition of many writers who, even after attaining renown, continued writing first for their neighbors.

Other pieces, notably those on the subject of the Holocaust, appeared in *Together,* the international publication for survivors. A few of the articles on Judaism were published in *The Reporter* newspaper of the Jewish community in New Hampshire. "Marrying into Memory" appeared first in *Moment* magazine. Several articles are based upon commentaries I delivered on National

Public Radio stations WBUR, Boston, and WEVO, Concord, New Hampshire. Other writings are original to this volume.

Norman Abelson
Concord, New Hampshire
March 2002

Kearsarge Mountain Books

Kearsarge Mountain Books is an imprint of the Writers Publishing Cooperative. The cooperative was organized to establish new relationships between writers, readers, and book sellers.

The Writers Publishing Cooperative is owned and operated by the writers whose books the co-op publishes.

Available from Kearsarge Mountain Books:

Poetry

Snapshots from a Love Affair by Norman Abelson

The Loggers of Warner by Roy Morrison

Telegrams from the Psych Ward by Marc Awodey

Mosaic II: Poems of an Ancient Order by Lester Hirsch

Cascadilla Creek by Zorika Petic

Fiction

Saint Michael's Letters to the Aesthesians by Michael J. Nedell

orders: call toll free 1-888-874-6904
www.essentialbooks.com